ASSUMPTIONS
OR
OVER-ASSUMPTIONS

Uday Basu is a senior journalist who has earned accolades both within the country and outside for his free, frank and fearless pen. He has worked for over four decades in the leading English daily *The Statesman*, serving the paper in different capacities and subsequently retiring as its Coordinating Editor. During his long career, he covered almost all aspects of public-social life, from administration, culture, education and crime to politics. His Op-Ed pieces on politics and other issues had a huge readership. He made a mark in international forums travelling to countries in Asia, Africa, Europe and the USA with his journalistic work. He was inducted as chairperson of the US-based International Association of Religion Journalists (IARJ). He has penned two books: *White Sahibs Brown Sahibs: An Insider's Account of The Statesman* (2024) and *Left Out in Bengal* (2012). Currently, he writes editorials for *Orissa Post*.

ASSUMPTIONS OR OVER-ASSUMPTIONS

THE STORY OF THE 2024 EXIT POLLS

UDAY BASU

Published by
Rupa Publications India Pvt. Ltd 2024
7/16, Ansari Road, Daryaganj
New Delhi 110002

Sales centres:

Bengaluru Chennai Hyderabad
Jaipur Kathmandu Kolkata
Mumbai Prayagraj

Copyright © Uday Basu 2024

The views and opinions expressed in this book are the author's own and the facts are as reported by them which have been verified to the extent possible, and the publishers are not in any way liable for the same.

All rights reserved.

No part of this publication may be reproduced, transmitted, or stored in a retrieval system, in any form or by any means, electronic, mechanical, photocopying, recording or otherwise, without the prior permission of the publisher.

P-ISBN: 978-93-6156-072-9
E-ISBN: 978-93-6156-476-5

First impression 2024

10 9 8 7 6 5 4 3 2 1

The moral right of the author has been asserted.

Printed in India

This book is sold subject to the condition that it shall not, by way of trade or otherwise, be lent, resold, hired out, or otherwise circulated, without the publisher's prior consent, in any form of binding or cover other than that in which it is published.

*To my father, the late professor Bibhuti Bhusan Basu,
who taught me the English language and how to read between the
lines in politics.
To my wife, Madhumita,
for standing by me in all my journalistic endeavours.
To my son, Abhimannyu,
for helping me meet the deadline for writing the book,
providing all laptop-related technical assistance.*

Contents

1. Dumbfounded: 4 June, 2024 — 1
2. Opening Pandora's Box: Lessons of 2004, 2009, 2019 — 15
3. Science Meets Social Science: The Theory of Exit Polls — 37
4. The Fallacy: Shocks of 2024 Indian Exit Polls — 71
5. Of Stocks and Shocks: The Economic Aftermath — 91
6. At the Helm of Our Fates: The ECI and the Message at Large — 105

Acknowledgements — 113

Notes — 115

Introduction

Imagine this: You are a wizard. Plus, a geeky character in a Christopher Nolan movie. Both combined in one soul.

For a day, a moment, you are given the power to rise high up in outer space and look down on the planet. You have been equipped with extraterrestrial powers, with a standing condition that you get to use these to fiddle around but not cause any damage (can't not leave humans with a word of caution, can we?). The view from up there is mesmerizing. After all this time, you actually understand what the physicists have been yammering about for years—the spectacle of our planet as a tiny speck in the larger scheme of the universe has never been clearer.

The geographical boundaries are clear as crystal and thanks to the likes of Elon Musk and Sundar Pichai, you have the option to look at the muggles and everything they are up to. For the sake of this story, let us assume that you are like me—someone interested in the politics of the world to a point of no return. In this scheme of things, you decide to use for a day the limited powers at your disposal and just for the fun

Assumptions or Over-Assumptions

of it, you create some ruckus. You turn up the chaos on the surface. But you don't want to harm anyone; you just wish to be mischievous and see what would happen if *that* happened. Because you are a political geek and an enthusiastic citizen of the globe, you want to see what the world would look like if it woke up and decided to vote, all on the same day. So, you flip the switch and suddenly the whole image of mortals going about their business changes. Suddenly, you see them forming what can only be considered the equivalent of the Great Wall of China. The media is scrambling, the diplomats are going haywire—if only the television had the bandwidth to show all the unintended coverage.

It is in this moment that you see, register and realize the magnitude of historical events. Due to that one image, elections suddenly seem to be *the* event—the only one that truly matters. The picture you have created shows you that these periodical exercises that come to the fore every four or five years have the single-largest effect on the future and fate of our planet. Getting them *right* is only the beginning of a long list of goals—effective policies, governance and administration, securing livelihoods, winning wars, combatting violence, and so on. Our lives depend on them. Due to their scattered timelines globally, we tend to create our own little bubbles where the idea of 'me, myself and I' seems to overtake the needs, demands and subjectivities of the larger population. One is compelled to wonder if there is a way to present this reality to the masses up close. Maybe then they would realize the true value of elections. Such events are

Introduction

beyond the scales of profits and losses. They are what our lives depend on.

Except, it's 2024. To an extent, this imagination is already a reality.

The Election Year

The *TIME* magazine's flare for drama was on full display in December 2023 when it observed that more than half of the world's total population would be heading to the polling booths the following year. The publication thus declared the current year, i.e. 2024, as 'the election year'.[1] The publication was not alone in its assessment. Its opinions were supported, echoed and highlighted when Staffan Lindberg, the director of the Swedish think tank Varieties of Democracy Institute, declared the sensational year to be the 'make-or-break year for democracy in the world'.[2] In a single year, approximately 4.2 billion citizens spread across almost 65 countries (plus the EU) are supposed to partake in elections.

The importance of these elections attains newer heights as we put these figures into context. Countries across the world are grappling with a range of issues. Rising authoritarianism, the curbing of individual rights and liberties, the mounting restrictions on the freedom of the press and an overall increase in anti-democratic values are just the many tips of a rather large and daunting iceberg.

The planet is in the midst of violent outbreaks, geopolitical

Assumptions or Over-Assumptions

tensions, climate change, a disintegrating global economy, and widening social and political inequities. As per contemporary media reports, ten most populous countries in the world will vote or have already voted this year. Eight of these ten, including the United States (US), Mexico and India, are continuing to face difficulties with ensuring voter participation, free speech and electoral independence.[3] Commentators, political scientists and media houses have been trying to claw their way through such countries in order to get insights, if any, into which way the wind is blowing.

The fear of democracy losing has become the topmost concern for anyone and everyone who cares about the political realities of our planet. Now more than ever, people are frantically trying to find authentic sources and reliable information that may help them decide who to vote for and what they wish to see as the future of national and global societies.

In the process, common citizens are relying more and more on the systems that work outside official electoral governance. The media and the pre- and post-poll exercises, worldwide, operate in a frenzy as they take on the Herculean task of giving their audiences a sneak peek into the results. For instance, much before the United Kingdom (UK) held the 2024 general elections, the opinion polls were already claiming that the British population were swaying the Labour way. On the other side of the world, claiming to be home to the world's oldest democracy, the US continues to take the pulse of potential voters. The country's media houses and

Introduction

publications are working round the clock to cover debates, conduct interviews and group discussions, and bring out reliable and insightful opinion polls before election-day voting in November.[4]

The zeal to predict and know what's next prevented the global media and society from limiting their attention to the West. The rattling chain of events of geopolitical importance in this part of the world forced them to look eastwards. The spectacle of the largest democracy on the planet voting has always held a special place in the eyes of the outsiders. Mere imagination is not enough to capture the reality of what it really takes to conduct elections in a country as large and diverse as our motherland, India.

Heavy is the Head that Wears the Crown

The Indian general elections have received the international community's somewhat undivided attention in the last few decades. Owing to her leaps of success, India has made an indelible mark in the past three decades. Given our country's key role in the global economy, the implications of how Indians vote matter much more than we might have anticipated.

For the international community, the most interesting aspect of contemporary Indian politics lies in the stark contradiction between a steadily growing economy and increasing social and political upheaval. Owing to these colourful contrasts, and the fact that they were happening

Assumptions or Over-Assumptions

with several other polls also underway this year worldwide, the Indian exit polls were closely watched and heavily discussed in the international media.

Given the high stakes and global interest around the results, we, as a country, should have collectively aimed at delivering flawless exit numbers. This was necessary not only for the sake of numerical accuracy but also because exit polls carry the essence of trust and faith in democracy and the pillars that keep it going. The possibility of wrong exit numbers shouldn't have even been the least of our options.

Yet the opposite happened.

On 1 June 2024, every major polling company's exit polls predicted a landslide victory for the incumbent party. They echoed, more or less, the same numbers as the Bharatiya Janata Party (BJP) had predicted for itself throughout its campaign. The most influential exit polls predicted that the party alone, and not the National Democratic Alliance (NDA), would beat its own record and secure more than 400 seats in the Indian parliament. The average predictions stood between 370 and 400 seats, while the main opposition front, the INDIA bloc, was predicted to wrap up its seat share below 200.[5] For a 543-seat parliament where majority rule is clocked at 50 per cent vote share, getting to the 272-seat mark would have been enough for the BJP. A 400-seat tally would make 'knocking it out of the park' an understatement. The stamp of approval from the exit polls was received with a varying range of emotions.

The ruling party thumped its chest and stood confident

Introduction

that the country was standing behind it. In what could be termed as a bit of an *over-assurance*, the leaders of the ruling BJP went on to make staggering remarks about the future of the country.

On the flip side, the INDIA bloc, wherein multiple opposition parties had joined forces to win the elections together, reacted strongly against the numbers. Some parties lashed out at the pollsters, while others challenged their predictions. The bloc came into existence when almost every opposition party joined hands to stand against what it claimed was an authoritarian regime of the BJP. The image of the Opposition suspended from the Winter Session of the Parliament[6] had sent shock waves across the country, alarming those who did not necessarily align with the BJP's politics and ideology.

In the middle was the general public. Some were ecstatic about the exit polls, while others could not help publicly expressing their disappointment. To the Leftists, the thought of the BJP securing a number as high as the one projected indicated that the nature of Indian democracy would change dramatically and drastically. The second scary outcome was that if these numbers materialized, the Opposition would be wiped out from the lower and upper houses and its relevance would die a public and historic death. The projections sent a chill down the spines of everyone who had experienced the Emergency era under the prime ministership of the Iron Lady of India, Indira Gandhi.

The international community also had an ambiguous response. While the leaders of many countries welcomed the

Assumptions or Over-Assumptions

projections, they did so largely because changes in political leadership are usually followed by disruptions in the work being done and relations made by the incumbent parties. A possible continued third term for the BJP meant that the countries could go about their business with India as usual. But for the watchdogs and critics of the BJP government, the exit polls painted a grey and worrying picture. Either way, 4 June 2024 was slowly creating its importance in the history of the Indian general elections.

As the sun rose on 3 June, a Monday, the Indian public, along with the rest of the world, was glued to their televisions, radios and websites, watching one of the most unexpected elections unfold.

To say that the numbers were off would be a grave understatement. The final tally saw the BJP stand at 240, the NDA at 286, and the INDIA bloc at an impressive 231 seats.[7]

Come 4 June 2024, the deception of the exit polls for the 2024 Indian general elections would catch the world by surprise. The headlines covering the elections could not help but report on the complete breakdown of the exit and opinion polling system of the country. The disappointing difference opened a can of worms, compelling us, the citizens, to revisit and re-evaluate past exit polls. When seen comparatively, they paint a worrisome picture for the status and future of Indian exit polls. This book attempts to piece together that story and offer a comprehensive take on the subject.

Introduction

Shrouded in Mystery

Over the years, exit polls in India have earned both fame and notoriety. Their existence begs a simple question—why can't people wait for two to three days after polling is over to get authentic results declared by the Election Commission of India (ECI)? Instead, why do they have to set store by exit poll results based on interviews of some samples of voters as they exit polling stations after casting their votes?

The purpose of exit polls is two-pronged. In one respect, exit polls can act as a source of primary data and insights about the qualitative aspects of elections, voter experience and the health of a democracy. This acts as a singular bank of information for academics, political analysts, psephologists and even political parties to analyse the ground realities of the electoral process and the mood of the electorate.

The second aspect or importance of exit polls comes from what it offers to citizens at large. In the modern age, which is now speedily transforming into the digital age, people have the ease and facility to know what is happening around them in a matter of a few clicks and seconds. Exit polls soothe anxious minds and enable them to stay in the loop of election news and updates.

Additionally, it allows the press and media to play a crucial role in the dance of democracy. It builds on the relationship that the Fourth Estate shares with the citizens. In India, as is the case in other countries, exit polls are conducted by different polling

Assumptions or Over-Assumptions

companies in collaboration with television news channels and media houses. This is done because the press and media alone are considered to be impartial standard-bearers of democracy and democratic values—the one pillar that is supposed to represent the voices of billions of citizens. Collaborating with the press, thus, is the polling companies' ultimate way to soothe the insatiable curiosity of the citizens.

In theory, the collaboration works in favour of curating reliable polls because the methodology of exit polls is such that there is no need to reach out to all the voters. The media, equipped with the task of reaching out to the masses, uses interviews of a section of voters spread across the country. With these crucial numbers at their disposal, the pollsters are supposed to have the wherewithal to compute near-accurate results. This is a boon of the political and social sciences as well as statistics. In addition to serving their core function, exit polls can also play an important role in strengthening democracy through a scientific study of voter psychology and voting patterns that provide invaluable data to voters for making informed choices of their representatives to form the government and work for their well-being.

However, the trends of the recent past reveal deep-seated cracks in the system. Indian exit polls, especially after their disastrous performance in 2024, have come under sharp criticism for their struggles with forecasting accurate election results. This event is indicative of the possibility that there could be serious flaws in the sampling of voters for, and the methodology

Introduction

of, interviews. The accuracy and accountability of exit polls have come under the scanner. After all, crafting the science of conducting reliable exit polls is a highly complex task which cannot include any shortcuts. The UK stands out as a shining example of having perfected this art and science of the exit polls. It has been predicting incredibly accurate results for nearly the past two decades. This has been possible because of two extraordinary minds in the country: political science professor Sir John Curtis and statistical wizard and professor David Firth.

I have been in journalism for over four decades. I have made countless pre-election surveys to understand voter psychology and assess which way the electoral wind blows at a particular point of time. Incidentally, the methodology that journalists like myself have often followed happens to be a key component of the technique the UK has been using for exit polls to produce results with what its modest pioneers call freakish accuracy.

However, the British model is difficult to apply in India because the UK has a two-party system that makes exit poll predictions easier, whereas India has a multi-party system. Plus, the Indian population is a heterogeneous mix of castes and ethnic groups, which further complicate exit poll forecasts.

However, this cannot be an excuse for churning out erroneous exit poll figures. If one has to be in the business of exit polls, one must enjoy the trust of the people and make the science and methodology credible. Equally, it would be wrong to abandon the exercise altogether in the event of consecutive failures. It would mean giving in to the factors that are causing us

Assumptions or Over-Assumptions

to decay from within and lose hope and trust in our institutions.

To prevent this loss of faith at a time when the Indian exit polls are really being put to the test, *Assumptions or Over-Assumptions* tries to find solutions by first acknowledging that a problem exists. That solves half the problem. The other half can be mitigated by our coming up with solutions collectively. Call it delusional optimism but there is some truth to the idea that where there is a will, there is a way.

ONE

Dumbfounded: 4 June, 2024

On 4 June 2024, India woke up with palpitations and an overpowering sense of excitement. After months of speeches, rallies and powerful campaigns, the contending political parties had put their fates in the hands of the Indian electorate. Over a period of six weeks, the Election Commission of India (ECI) remained on its toes as it yet again showcased to the world its tenacity and efficiency in conducting the world's largest election.[8] Indians had diligently performed their civic duty and cast their votes—each doing their bit to decide the fate of the political elites and their affiliations and the future of the country at large. All eyes, now, were on the apex authority on elections in India to announce the much-awaited results.

The day started early for the ECI, journalists and political pundits. Counting began at 8.00 a.m. in the morning and no one knew when this long day would end. However, there was a

Assumptions or Over-Assumptions

general consensus about how it would end courtesy of the exit polls that had been announced two days earlier.

On that eventful morning, the dominant pollsters, more than any other sect, were confident of their predictions. The optimism and sheer faith in their projections had earned them seats in the country's leading newsrooms as 'experts' who had beaten the ECI to announce the results.

By the turn of the day, as dusk descended, the entire scene had changed. The sight of a leading pollster from a poll prediction company, which conducts exit polls, breaking down and crying inconsolably on a live television programme before the national audience after his poll predictions for the 2024 Lok Sabha elections proved horribly wrong was certainly not an edifying spectacle—and yet what would become an iconic image in the minds of the Indian public. The unbelievable had happened. Against their thumping tallies, the 2024 Indian general election results proved yet again that the Indian electorate remains unpredictable, a mystery that these pollsters and media houses cannot seem to figure out. Simply put, the projections were way off. Axis My India had projected that the incumbent party would return to power with a majority of more than 400 seats, while the Opposition would not even reach a decent 200-seat mark. It was not alone in declaring these numbers. The pollster in question was so devastated by the company's failure to get the numbers right that even prompt help from the television anchor of the show to console him and wipe his tears was of no avail.[9] The scene was so effective that

Dumbfounded: 4 June, 2024

even the international media could not help but highlight the man breaking down. The nation watched it with utter disbelief and dismay as the credibility of the Indian exit polls came under the scanner globally.

Why was the pollster so shaken? Was he feeling guilty that he had let the voters down and that his goodwill was in tatters? Was it an attempt to win people's sympathy by a man who deals with hard, cold statistics that are supposed to be used for arriving at objective, dispassionate conclusions? Was it an admission of the failure of the latest technique and art of delving into the social psyche of the electorate?

While the image and the shocking results prompted an array of questions, they also did something more. They forced us, the viewers, to revisit and re-evaluate the past performance of our exit pollsters and the accuracy of their projections. Indian pollsters and television anchors presenting exit poll results have so often had to eat dust and hang their heads in shame for making terribly wrong poll predictions that their inefficacy became normalized for a period of almost two decades. Yet, 2024 turned out to be their graveyard.

The Backdrop

India occupies a great position in the comity of nations for its track record of upholding democratic values since winning independence from British rule in 1947. In what has become one of the most crucial components of democracy, the country

Assumptions or Over-Assumptions

has been successfully undertaking the exercise of the transfer of power from one political party to another or a coalition with the help of the ballot and not the bullet, as has been the practice in many countries in Asia, Africa and elsewhere after winning freedom from the shackles of colonial rule.

Elections are central to the functioning of democracy. They are not merely an exercise in which eligible voters queue up before polling booths in a 'carnival spirit' and stamp on the ballot or press the button on electronic voting machines (EVMs) as part of what is so erroneously and mischievously called 'a festival of democracy'. Far from it, elections are a very serious matter. They are the means of making a political choice by voting. Elections are an integral part of democracy in that they give citizens a direct opportunity to make their political choice and have a say in the governance of the country by selecting their preferred leaders and parties for handling issues of public concern and managing the country in the interest of the people. Therefore, it is safe to say that elections play a crucial role for the stability and development of democracy. They constitute a mechanism through which modern democracy operates.

In the last century, another medium has emerged to support and examine elections in our country. It is yet another product of the West that has been implemented worldwide and involves various stakeholders who study, assess and project the opinion of the masses. It has come to be known to the general public as pre-election and post-election polls—namely, the opinion and exit polls respectively.

Dumbfounded: 4 June, 2024

There is a marked difference between exit polls and opinion polls. Through opinion polls, the surveyors seek to understand whom voters plan to vote for. A demographic study, comparative estimates of the seats won in previous elections, and the addition of new voters to different constituencies are taken into consideration for opinion polls. On the other hand, exit polls, as the term suggests, imply a sample study of voters exiting polling stations right after casting their votes. The surveyors try to gauge the voters' outlook and whom they actually voted for. On the basis of their responses, statistical modules are used to predict the number of seats the contesting parties may win or lose. The whole exercise is done with the help of several branches of science: political science, social science and statistics.

Exit polls in India are governed by the ECI's provisions. Under Section 126 of the amended Representation of the People (Amendment) Act, 1996, the ECI imposes certain restrictions on the publication of exit polls in order to ensure that voters are not in any way influenced in exercising their franchise. Section 126 prohibits—apart from holding, convening or attending any public meeting or procession—displaying to the public any election matter by means of cinematography, television or other similar apparatus 'during the period of 48 hours ending with the hour fixed for the conclusion of the poll'. The contravention of the prohibition is an offence punishable with imprisonment up to two years or with fine or with both.[10]

The law is thus clear that the voter needs a period of at

Assumptions or Over-Assumptions

least 48 hours before the completion of the poll, during which he should not be disturbed in the process of weighing the merits and demerits of the political parties and the contesting candidates in the electoral fray, in a peaceful, quiet and balanced frame of mind.

At the same time, the ECI attaches due importance to the freedom of the press in a democratic country and the rights of print and electronic media to gather information on any issue or event of public importance, and disseminate it to the general public for their information and decision-making. Nevertheless, it does not give unfettered freedom to the media and maintains a balance between such rights of the press and the rights of the electorate in the matter of the exercise of their franchise in a free and fair manner, unencumbered by any extraneous factors. It is acceptable that while striking such a balance, it would not be unreasonable and unfair for the ECI to put certain reasonable restrictions on the dissemination of information.

With the revolutionary development of technology, the science and art of holding elections have undergone a sea change over the years. The media, political scientists, statistics experts and voters have now teamed up to attempt to predict election results through opinion polls and, most importantly, exit polls. Equipped with the latest technology, voters today are in a position to compare and contrast how fellow citizens living in the farthest corner of the country, thousands of miles away from their homes, feel about the suitability, or the lack thereof, of the crop of political leaders and parties who are in the fray.

Dumbfounded: 4 June, 2024

A sort of herd psychology develops in this process, making it easier than before for voters across the country to decide on the political representatives they want to send to parliament to run the government.

This opens up a brave new world of studying voter psychology, poll predictions and exit polls, as well as the emergence of a new genre of hybrid journalism in which psephologists and the media collaborate, making the most of what is known as TRP (television rating point) culture, with warts and all, merits and demerits.

Earlier, in the absence of effective communication channels, voters were generally clueless about the views of the electorate residing in other parts of the country. They had a myopic view of the situation and decision-making largely remained localized, restricted to a village, town, district or, at the most, state. The practice continued till the early 1990s, with interactions between journalists, election surveyors and voters being too narrow and limited in scope. This is why the media at the time, by and large, stopped short of making predictions about the number of seats the contending political parties could win. Instead, their focus was on understanding the mood of the electorate on the basis of the performance—or non-performance—of the incumbent government and offering broad indications about the choice the voters might make on the polling day. Whenever I toured different parts of the country for such pre-election analyses during my long career in journalism spanning over four decades, my unambiguous brief from my bosses was that I would not,

Assumptions or Over-Assumptions

under any circumstances, try to predict the number of seats the political parties might end up getting.

The print media then had no pretentions that *their* forecasts might be closest to reality. They simply did not have the manpower, resources, network and technology to do so. Even landline phones were a luxury then. Hence, they were unabashed in admitting their shortcomings and limitations by stopping short of hazarding any guesses about the seats to be won or lost. However, with the arrival of smartphones and social media, poll predictions in India are now a different ball game altogether since people can connect with each other, at a national or even global level, in a fraction of a second. The reach of the new technologies in this regard can be gauged from the latest statistics.

Taking advantage of the phenomenal progress of digital technology, a plethora of companies have mushroomed, forming a sort of poll prediction industry or syndicate. This is indeed a fascinating development that makes the traditional methods of election surveys and pre-poll analyses, which were followed by the print media for decades till the 1990s, seem like something belonging to the bullock-cart age. However, as things go scandalously wrong today for the accuracy and authenticity of poll forecasts using new technologies, the value of the methodology followed by the print media in the past cannot be denied.

Dumbfounded: 4 June, 2024

The Entry of the Exits

In India, among the private companies that have become almost household names for trying to map voter psychology and predict election results before they are officially declared by the ECI are Axis My India, CVoter, Today's Chanakya, CNX, ETG, Matrize, AC Nielsen, Hansa Research and CSDS. There are several others as well that are in the business. These companies have tie-up arrangements with notable 24-hour television news channels such as Times Now, India Today, Zee News, ABP News, Republic TV, India TV, News 18 and CNN-IBN.

However, India has a very short history of opinion and exit polls. Even though the concept is growing progressively and catching the popular imagination fast, India is decidedly far behind the West in this regard. The rate of failure in predicting general elections results is quite high despite stray successes in the case of some state assembly elections here and there. This is because the Indian situation is far more complex than that of the West, where the success rate is encouraging as the degree of homogeneity is much higher and the two-party system is in vogue. In contrast, India has a multi-party system and its society is heterogeneous. Notwithstanding this reality, Indian poll prediction companies are doing a better job than those of some other Third World countries.

The first national poll in India was carried out by the Indian Institute of Public Opinion (IIPO) before the 1957 general elections. It was headed by Eric da Costa, who is considered

Assumptions or Over-Assumptions

the father of opinion polling in India.[11] He was an economist and a journalist. The IIPO has covered almost all elections since then. Eric, as he was popularly known, experimented with his multiplier theory during the 1957 election. But the module he used turned out to be not so effective and suffered decline in the course of time.

It was the news magazine *India Today* that launched proper opinion polls in India in 1980 when it commissioned IMRB with Ashok Lahiri and Prannoy Roy, economist-cum-psephologist-cum-journalist, to conduct the first-ever pan-India survey. With the help of the research agency MARG and Prannoy Roy, it conducted opinion polls with a great degree of success during the general elections of 1984, 1989, 1991, 1996, 1998, 1999, and so on, all the way till 2014.[12]

The underlying principle of exit polls is that voting patterns are essentially traced by combining number crunching with insights into voter psychology (i.e., how one behaves or how the human mind works in a particular situation). The human mind functions differently in different situations, dictated by its needs, the influence exerted by its surroundings, and its affinities with fellow beings. The outcome of the voter's thought process is largely shaped by these factors. This explains why election results often come as a rude shock to those who sit in the comfort zone of TV studios in capital cities, far removed from the real mood of the nation. Often, they overestimate the relevance of the sentiments of a smaller representative group within their access and conclude that it reflects what the larger, actual voting population feels. That is what makes or mars exit polls.

The data collected during exit polls is analysed and then pollsters come to definite conclusions with a small, permissible margin of error. There is no room in exit polls for speculating about voters' preferences since their response is sought only after they have made up their minds and decided on the electoral fortunes of the candidates and their parties. Pollsters—usually, private companies working for newspapers and television channels—conduct exit polls to gain an early indication of how an election went.

Voting behaviour is essentially a mental and physical activity. It is the individual voter who chooses the ruler and, at the same time, gives their assessment of decision-making in the immediate past. The impact of opinion polls and exit polls in shaping this voting behaviour during elections is a matter of contentious debate. Critics of the practice opine that any kind of influence on voters may be regarded as a poor way of their exercising a democratic choice even if opinion polls and exit polls used for the purpose are accurate.

For this reason, some psephologists and academics are not happy with the way exit polls are conducted by established poll prediction companies in collaboration with television channels and other media outlets. The former group believes that both the methodology and intent of the poll forecasting companies are suspect. For academicians and members of the political science community, exit polls can be a unique source to understand a lot more than just whom voters vote for. The essence of exit polls

Assumptions or Over-Assumptions

can help capture voters' experiences and act as a solid feedback mechanism for not just political parties but also the election commissions. The lack of this nuance in our present-day exit polls is borne out by the fact that exit poll predictions have, over the years, been turning out to be flop shows.[13]

In India, the scientific study of elections, called psephology, began as an academic exercise at the Centre for the Study of Developing Societies (CSDS), Delhi, in the 1960s.[14] Its primary focus was to study the voting behaviour and attitudes of voters. It is indeed a great tool to understand the minds of voters and how socio-economic factors influence their electoral choices. This way, psephology becomes a powerful tool to strengthen democracy. Over the years, the field has become equated with pre-poll surveys and exit polls, which are conducted by almost all major media houses to predict the winners of various elections.

Election surveys, whether pre-poll or post-poll, are based on a random sample drawn from the ECI's voter list. These are generally accurate, as they rely on a representative sample which rules out coverage errors and minimizes sampling errors. On the other hand, exit polls, done on the day of elections, are based on what is known as quota or purposive sampling.[15] As such, they run the risk of completely leaving out some sections and sub-samples of the population. Thus, the sample frame of exit polls is unrepresentative in most cases. It is fraught with both coverage and sampling errors.

Yogendra Yadav, a well-known psephologist, has been sticking out his neck for the past few years for the purpose

Dumbfounded: 4 June, 2024

of course correction, earning accolades for his acumen in the field. He maintains that there is no guarantee that a bigger sample size will ensure the right result. On the contrary, he argues that bigger surveys used by established poll prediction companies multiply errors by ten times.[16] The method of sampling used in an election survey and its accuracy also play an important role in making a reasonably accurate election forecast. Thus, a smaller representative sample can help make an accurate prediction as compared to a bigger unrepresentative sample. The method of sampling used in surveys conducted by market research organizations is usually criticized for not being scientific enough. This becomes clear when measuring the voting preferences and intentions of people from various castes and communities.

For one thing, general elections in India are a mammoth exercise in which tens of millions of people participate. No other country that has adopted the democratic form of government can match India on this score. The number of voters is increasing by leaps and bounds every year, making the whole process more and more complex while throwing up new challenges to both pollsters and media outlets.

The battle between established exit poll companies, on the one hand, and well-known political scientists, psephologists and agencies (such as Yogendra Yadav, Prannoy Roy and CSDS), on the other, continues because of the successive failures of exit polls in predicting at least near-accurate Lok Sabha election results in the years 2004, 2009, 2014, 2019 and, finally, 2024.

Assumptions or Over-Assumptions

This has thoroughly exposed the lack of proper expertise of those in the exit poll business.

Over the past two decades, Indian exit polls have had a rather unenviable track record. It was expected after the brouhaha over the new tools of election results that a battery of statisticians, political and social scientists, and seasoned journalists working in tandem would produce figures that, while not fully accurate, would at least be close to the official tally. The acceptable margin of error globally, as articulated by pollsters with established credentials, is 3 per cent.[17] If this target is not met, the efficacy, utility and credibility of exit polls come under a big question mark.

Keeping this basic aim in view, an examination of India's Lok Sabha exit poll results over the past two decades would be instructive.

TWO

Opening Pandora's Box: Lessons of 2004, 2009, 2019

In 2004, the Atal Bihari Vajpayee-led Bharatiya Janata Party (BJP) government called for early elections, buoyed as it was by victories in Madhya Pradesh, Chhattisgarh and Rajasthan. It coined the catchy slogan 'India Shining' and launched a massive country-wide campaign with the message that the government had brought about stupendous qualitative changes in the life of the common man in the country.[1] Hype was created to such an extent that it was compared with Indira Gandhi's poll campaign of *Garibi Hatao* ('eradicate poverty') that ran from the late 1960s to the early 1970s.

In 2004, the general elections were held in four phases between 20 April and 10 May. Over 670 million people were eligible to vote and elect 543 members of the 14th Lok Sabha.[2] Seven states also held assembly elections to elect state governments. These were the first elections in India that were carried out using electronic voting machines (EVMs) all the way through.[3] According to the ECI, over 370 million voters, out of 675 million eligible citizens, voted. The average number of enrolment of new voters in each constituency was 1.2 million, although the largest constituency had 3.1 million.[4]

In these elections, compared to all the Lok Sabha elections of the 1990s, the battle was more of a direct contest between two blocs, in the sense that there was no viable third front alternative. Largely, the contest was between the BJP and its allies, on the one hand, and the Indian National Congress and its allies, on the other. The situation did, however, show large regional differences.

The BJP fought the elections as part of the National Democratic Alliance (NDA), though some of its seat-sharing arrangements were made with strong regional parties outside the NDA, such as the Telugu Desam Party (TDP) in Andhra Pradesh and the All India Anna Dravida Munnetra Kazhagam (AIADMK) in Tamil Nadu.

Ahead of the elections, there were attempts to form a Congress-led national-level joint opposition front. In the end, an agreement could not be reached, but regional-level alliances between the Congress and regional parties were made in several states. This was the first time that the Congress contested with those types of alliances in a parliamentary election. The Left parties—most notably, the Communist Party of India (Marxist) (the CPI-M) and the Communist Party of India (the CPI)—contested on their own in their strongholds in the three states of West Bengal, Kerala and Tripura, confronting both the Congress and the NDA. In several other states, such as Punjab and Andhra Pradesh, they clinched seat-sharing deals with the Congress. In Tamil Nadu, they were part of the DMK-led Democratic Progressive Alliance. Two parties refused to go along with either the Congress or the BJP: the Bahujan Samaj Party (BSP) and the Samajwadi Party (SP), both based in Uttar Pradesh (UP).

Most analysts believed that the NDA would win the elections. This assessment was also supported by the opinion polls.[5] The economy had shown steady growth in the past few months and the disinvestment of government-owned production units was on track. India's foreign exchange reserves stood at more than US$100 billion, estimated to be the seventh largest in the world and a record for India. The service sector had also generated a lot of jobs.[6] The party was supposed to have been riding on a wave of the so-called 'feel-good factor', typified by its 'India Shining' campaign.

In the past, the BJP had largely projected itself as a right-wing Hindu party linked with hard-line Hindutva organizations such as the Rashtriya Swayamsevak Sangh (RSS) and the Vishva Hindu Parishad (VHP). However, under Vajpayee, the party had slightly distanced itself from its hard-line ideology in order to accommodate a variety of other parties within the NDA, such as the Trinamool Congress (a Congress breakaway party) and breakaway factions of the Janata Dal, like the JD(U), the Biju Janata Dal (BJD) of Orissa (now Odisha), and the AIADMK. The soft Hindutva embraced by Vajpayee was, however, questioned after the party's poor showing in the assembly elections. These elections were marked by the campaign's emphasis on economic gains. Over the past few elections, the BJP had realized that its voter base had reached a saturation point, which prompted it to go for pre-poll rather than post-poll alliances.

Against this backdrop, pollsters went about with their task of conducting opinion polls and exit polls, proclaiming a thumping victory for the ruling NDA. Likewise, poll prediction companies announced their exit poll results.[7]

TABLE 2.1
2004 Exit Polls

Polling organization	NDA	UPA	Other
NDTV-AC Nielsen	230-250	190-205	100-120
Star News-C voter	263-275	174-184	86-98
Aaj Tak-MARG	248	190	105
Actual result	**181**	**218**	**Left Front-59**

When the actual results were announced on 13 May, the bubble of the exit polls burst, sending shockwaves across poll pundits and their promoters, i.e., different media houses. The final official tally was completely different from the exit poll figures. The NDA was far below the magic number of 272 seats. It managed to win 181 seats. The UPA notched up 218 seats, a far greater number than the exit poll companies had allowed it. The exit poll projections for other parties also went haywire. These parties won among themselves 143 seats as opposed to the projected maximum of 100 to 120.[8]

The Congress, which had governed India for all but five years from Independence until 1996, returned to power in 2004 after a record eight years out of office. It was able to put together a comfortable majority of more than 335 members out of 543 with the help of its allies. The 335 members included both the Congress-led United Progressive Alliance (UPA), the governing coalition formed after the election, and external support from the BSP, the SP, Kerala Congress (KC) and the Left Front.

The 2009 Chapter

The second stint came during the Lok Sabha elections of 2009. The election was held under extraordinary circumstances as the Left bloc, which had supported the ruling UPA government with its solid tally of 59 seats, had pulled out of the government on the controversial issue of the operationalization of the Indo-US civilian nuclear deal in 2008.[9] There was internal dissension within the CPI-M. Its general secretary, Prakash Karat, was vehemently opposed to the deal, while most of the comrades from Bengal and the second-in-command of the party, Sitaram Yechury, preferred a soft stand on the issue. The latter group feared that toppling the government on this issue, as advocated

Assumptions or Over-Assumptions

by Karat and his comrades from his state (Kerala), would be suicidal.

The crucial nuclear deal was on the point of being torpedoed. Karat travelled to different parts of the country explaining to the people that the nuclear deal was but a quid pro quo. It would open the floodgates for the sale of US military hardware, worth billions of dollars, to India. That would bring three cheers to the US military strategy on the Indian Ocean.

He went into the economics of the production of nuclear energy, especially its cost-benefit ratio compared to that of thermal power generation. He also sought to touch patriotic chords by raising the question of the Centre's tardy progress in the exploration and production of thorium, which would reduce the dependence on nuclear energy.

The Congress leadership and seasoned diplomats went ahead, on government instructions, with signing the deal and carrying out the process to its logical conclusion, all the while pretending that the government would get a 'sense' of the parliament's view before doing anything. The Left parties were lulled into the belief that the debate would continue for over a year and that by such time, the Indo-US nuclear deal would fall through, as the tenure of the Bush presidency would be over.

Karat and his comrades, however, had the shock of their lives when, on 7 July 2008, Prime Minister Manmohan Singh asserted, onboard a special aircraft en route to Japan for attending the G-8 Summit, that the government would 'very soon' approach the International Atomic Energy Agency (IAEA) for the operationalization of the nuclear deal. The very next day, the Left, led by Karat, declared the withdrawal of its support from the UPA government.[10]

The Manmohan Singh regime was unfazed and it announced it had the required number that would ensure the government did not collapse. On that very day, the SP announced its support to the UPA government and that it would hand over a fresh letter of support to the President the following day. The Left moved no-confidence and the government survived, as it did have the required numbers. The government went back to business as usual even though its equations with the second-largest bloc in the Lok Sabha—the Left—had got ruptured.

The government lasted its full term and then the elections were held in due course.

The 2009 elections adopted re-drawn electoral constituencies based on the 2001 Census following the 2002 Delimitation Commission of India, whose recommendations had been approved in February 2008.[11]

In the 2009 general elections, 499 out of the total 543 parliamentary constituencies were newly delimited constituencies. This affected the National Capital Region (NCR), the Union Territory of Puducherry, and all states except Arunachal Pradesh, Assam, Jammu & Kashmir, Jharkhand, Manipur and Nagaland. It is important to note that while comparing election results, it must be borne in mind that in many instances, a constituency with the same name as a state may reflect a significantly different

Assumptions or Over-Assumptions

population demographic as well as a slightly altered geographical region compared to that of the state.

Before the elections could start, the ECI got involved in a controversy due to internal problems. On 31 January 2009, the Chief Election Commissioner (CEC), N Gopalaswami, recommended to President Pratibha Patil that Navin Chawla, one of the Election Commissioners (ECs), be sacked for behaving in a partisan manner.[12] It was unclear if the CEC had the legal and constitutional right to provide such a unilateral recommendation. Chawla refused to resign, as he was expected to take over the post of CEC a few months later.

This controversy also resulted in the speculation that the ECI was unable to agree on the actual polling dates, with the incumbent CEC, Gopalaswami, preferring that at least one phase of the elections be held before his retirement on 20 April 2009. Navin Chawla, on the other hand, wanted the elections to start only after Gopalaswami had retired.

Eventually, on 1 March 2009, President Patil rejected Gopalaswami's recommendation to remove Chawla after the government advised her to do so.[13] Soon after the presidential announcement, the ECs got together and decided on the poll schedule.

The 2009 general elections saw three main national pre-poll alliances. The two larger blocs—the UPA and the NDA—had clearly indicated their prime ministerial candidates during the campaign for the elections. The Third Front announced that their prime ministerial candidate would be decided after the

Opening Pandora's Box: Lessons of 2004, 2009, 2019

election results were out. In the Indian parliamentary system, the announcement of the prime ministerial candidates is not necessary prior to the elections.

The UPA had been formed after the 2004 general elections to bring together parties that either allied with the Congress in various states or were willing to support a Congress-led national government. The main Opposition party, the BJP, along with its NDA coalition partners, had announced on 11 December 2007—more than a year before the elections—that their prime ministerial candidate would be BJP party leader L.K. Advani. On 23 January 2008, NDA leaders convened a meeting in the capital to officially elect him as their candidate for the election.

The newly formed Third Front alliance represented 109 seats before the 2009 election. The CPI-M-led Third Front was essentially a collection of regional political parties which were neither in the UPA nor in the NDA. Along with it, the Fourth Front was also formed before the 2009 elections, after the SP, Rashtriya Janata Dal (RJD) and Lok Janshakti Party (LJP) failed to reach seat-sharing agreements with the Congress. The Fourth Front hoped to play the kingmaker's role after the elections. However, it continued to declare its support for the UPA.[14]

The Congress was upbeat despite its frictions with the Left. It launched an innovative campaign and bought the rights for the Oscar-winning soundtrack 'Jai Ho' from the movie *Slumdog Millionaire* (2008), which was used as the official campaign tune by the party. The Congress calculated that the popular song would galvanize the masses during the almost month-long election season.

Its manifesto highlighted all the achievements of the UPA government over the past five years that it had been in power and identified various policies to be improved to further favour rural and underprivileged sections of Indian society.

However, the Congress campaign ran into trouble when the ECI took exception to a full-page advertisement around the 2010 Commonwealth Games published in major Delhi newspapers. The ECI served notice to the concerned ministry and the Cabinet Secretary and the Chief Secretary of Delhi, stating that the advertisement was a clear violation of the Model Code of Conduct (MCC) since it enumerated the achievements of the UPA government.[15] The ECI also asked the violators to pay penalties out of their own pockets.

The BJP manifesto took on the UPA government on three fronts—good governance, development and security. It highlighted all the different NDA policies that the UPA had reversed over the past five years. The manifesto underscored the importance of strong anti-terrorism laws and vowed to make India a safer place if the NDA was voted to power.

The BJP campaign faced its biggest controversy when the ECI directed the District Magistrate (DM) of Pilbhit to lodge a criminal case against BJP candidate Varun Gandhi for his allegedly inflammatory speech against minority communities made on 7 March 2009.[16] The ECI found Varun Gandhi guilty of violating the MCC by creating a feeling of enmity and hatred

Opening Pandora's Box: Lessons of 2004, 2009, 2019

between different communities, and issued a recommendation to the BJP to drop him from their list of candidates. The BJP, however, rallied behind Gandhi and refused to oblige the ECI.

One interesting feature of the election campaigns of all the contenders was the widespread use of the new technology of sending voice messages to voters so as to reach out to them without going to them physically. Although SMS had been used during prior elections too, political parties were now realizing that rural and illiterate voters, which formed the majority of the electorate, could not read. Young and tech-savvy politicians quickly understood that audio was the ideal way to reach out to the rural community and speak their language, so to say. This turned out to be very interesting, as two voice companies from India, TringMe and VoiceHaw, played a pivotal role in reaching out to the billion rural people of India.[17]

Against this backdrop, most opinion polls conducted by major agencies gave the UPA an edge over the NDA but neither of the blocs was predicted to get absolute majority. A few of them, however, forecast that the UPA, with the help of the Fourth Front, was to secure seats close to a majority. The opinion polls reckoned that other regional parties would play an important role by winning a substantial number of seats.

TABLE 2.2
2009 Pre-Poll Surveys

Agency	Dates	Results		
		UPA	NDA	Others
CNN-IBN-CSDS[18]	8 January–15 September	215–235	165–185	125–155
Star-Nielsen[19]	5 March–17 March	257 (Congress 144)	184 (BJP 137)	96 (Third Front)
CVoter–*The Week*[20]	March–April	234 (Congress 144)	186 (BJP 140)	112 (Third Front)
The Times of India[21]	March	201 (Congress 146)	195 (BJP 138)	147

An interesting development took place in February 2009 when the ECI banned the publication of all exit polls starting 48 hours before Phase 1 of the elections until the end of Phase 5.[22] This was intended to prevent the exit polls conducted in earlier phases from affecting voter decisions in later phases. The ban ended with the close of Phase 5 of voting at 5.00 p.m. IST on 13 May. The exit poll prediction companies released their numbers on the appointed date and hour.[23]

Opening Pandora's Box: Lessons of 2004, 2009, 2019

TABLE 2.3
2009 Exit Polls

Polling organization	UPA	NDA
CNN-IBN–*Dainik Bhaskar*	195	175
India TV-CVoter	195	189
Star-Nielsen	199	196
Headlines Today	191	180
Actual result	262	158

As in the 2004 Lok Sabha elections, the elections in 2009 also defied the predictions made by pre-poll surveys and exit polls, giving a new mandate for the incumbent UPA government. The exit polls failed to estimate the saturation of caste-based identity politics, the focus on good governance, and the BJP's limitations. Another factor that contributed to the Congress-led UPA's victory, which the exit polls could not properly assess in their analyses, was the vote-splitting by regional parties, such as the BSP and the MNS in Maharashtra, which helped the Congress gain many of its seats.

The 2014 Chapter

The Lok Sabha elections in 2014 marked a watershed moment in India's electoral politics with the unprecedented rise of the BJP under the leadership of Narendra Modi, who rose from the position of Chief Minister of Gujarat to become the Prime Minister of India. As Chief Minister, he had already become

Assumptions or Over-Assumptions

an international figure for all the wrong reasons. He had been warned in 2002 by his own party boss, the then Prime Minister Atal Bihari Vajpayee, about his failure to perform what the PM termed *raj dharma* during the riots and the persecution of minorities in his state.

Once again, the exit poll companies failed miserably to gauge the mood of the voters and predict the results accurately.

The 2014 general elections were held in nine phases from 7 April to 12 May 2014. A total of 8,251 candidates contested the 543 Lok Sabha seats.[24][25] The average election turnout over all the nine phases was around 66.40 per cent, the highest ever in the history of India's general elections.[26]

The election was fought against the backdrop of an unprecedented anti-corruption movement launched by social activist Anna Hazare and other similar moves by former IRS official Arvind Kejriwal. Kejriwal went on to form a separate political party, the Aam Aadmi Party (AAP), in November 2012.

Apart from the issue of alleged monumental corruption under the incumbent government, what agitated the people was unemployment, high inflation, economic slowdown, security concerns, terrorism, religious strife, communalism, as well as poor road, water and power infrastructure.

An impression was created in the minds of the voters that Prime Minister Manmohan Singh was an ineffectual angel—an 'accidental prime minister'. The description stuck in popular perception after a book with the same title was published before the 2014 Lok Sabha polls. Penguin India's *The Accidental Prime*

Opening Pandora's Box: Lessons of 2004, 2009, 2019

Minister: The Making and Unmaking of Manmohan Singh was authored by Sanjaya Baru, who had earlier left a successful career as chief editor of the *Financial Express* to join Prime Minister Manmohan Singh as his media adviser in UPA-I. Singh offered him the job with the words that as PM, he would be isolated from the outside world and for this, he wanted Baru to be his 'eyes and ears'. He also asked Baru to tell him whatever he thought the PM should know, without fear or favour.[27]

Baru's book threw light on the behind-the-scene activities during Manmohan Singh's regime. His account appeared credible enough because he had inside information. The book threw light on what its blurb claimed were 'Singh's troubled relations with his ministers and cautious equation with Sonia Gandhi'. Through Baru's narrative, Indian citizens came to know about, for the first time, Singh's plight in heading a government which supposedly had two power centres.

The Opposition, which later campaigned against the so-called policy paralysis of the UPA-II regime, was buttressed by the revelations in the book that seemed to strike a chord with people. In the summer of 2013, the current account deficit and a falling rupee aptly reflected the state of the country's economy. The BJP launched a widespread campaign stating that the lack of a clear mandate could lead to a serious economic situation that would greatly harm the common man. The price of onions, a staple in Indian cuisine, faced a dramatic increase. In the lead-up to the elections, consumer price inflation increased more than expected, while industrial production fell sharply. The rise in

Assumptions or Over-Assumptions

the price of salt served as a vivid picture to the common man of the level of general food inflation in the country.

At the time of the UPA-II government, a number of scams came to public attention, tarnishing the image of the government among common citizens. Of these, the most shocking scam that captured the imagination of the people was the 2G Spectrum case. There were scams galore, such as the Coal scam, the Augusta Westland chopper scam, and the Commonwealth Games scam.

The BJP manifesto promised to set up the Price Stabilization Fund and the National Agriculture Market to check price rise, to promote electronic and policy-driven governance, and to simplify the tax regime to prevent corruption. It sought to encourage labour-intensive manufacturing, focus on traditional employment bases of agriculture, upgrade infrastructure and housing, and provide self-employment opportunities for job creation. Harnessing satellite technology, setting up the National Optical-Fibre Network up to the village level, and launching the Diamond Quadrilateral project to establish a high-speed train network were among several other things that the party promised.

Modi's 'masterstroke' during the election campaign was the promise, at a rally in Gurgaon (officially known as Gurugram), that he would fix the problems 'perpetuated by the Congress for 60 years in just 60 months,' and prove that the BJP was the 'best option' for India.[28]

He also sought to portray the Gandhi family as a fountainhead of corruption and alleged that the Congress was protecting Robert Vadra, the son-in-law of Sonia Gandhi, after he had 'sold farmers' land and made money off it'. 'Robert Vadra's empty bank account was credited with US$8.3 million (INR 500 million) in just three months. BJP wants answers,' he demanded.[29] He also criticized Nandan Nilekani for the preparation of Aadhaar cards for millions of people, which even the Supreme Court questioned on the grounds that it did not address security concerns.

In this climate, the BJP campaign slogan *Ab Ki Baar, Modi Sarkar* ('this time, a Modi government') seemed to have great traction among the millions of voters. Modi also tried to lambast the UPA-II government on its foreign policy, portraying the Prime Minister as too meek a leader to really take on an aggressive China breathing down India's neck in the eastern flank. The cumulative effects of the campaigns were such that the 2014 general elections turned out to be an unprecedented disaster for the UPA, as the alliance garnered the lowest number of seats in its history.

Most of the exit polls foresaw the BJP-led NDA coming to power but completely failed to predict the landslide victory of the alliance.

Here is a breakdown of the exit poll numbers[30]:

Predictions on NDA

1. India Today-Cicero: 272 seats
2. News 24-Chanakya: 340 seats
3. CNN-IBN-CSDS: 280 seats

Assumptions or Over-Assumptions

4. Times Now ORG: 249 seats
5. ABP News-Nielsen: 274 seats
6. NDTV-Hansa Research: 279 seats

Predictions on UPA

1. India Today-Cicero: 115 seats
2. News 24-Chanakya: 101 seats
3. CNN-IBN-CSDS: 97 seats
4. Times Now ORG: 148 seats
5. ABP News-Nielsen: 97 seats
6. NDTV-Hansa Research: 103 seats

Actual results

NDA: 336 seats; BJP won 282 seats
UPA: 60 seats; Congress won just 44 seats

The exit poll companies did not secure glory with their poll predictions for the 2019 Lok Sabha elections either. The margin of error between the forecasts and the actual results was far beyond the acceptable limit of five to 15 seats.

The same is illustrated by the following comparison:

1. **CVoter:** 287 for NDA, 128 for the UPA, and the remaining seats for other parties.
2. **News24-Todays Chanakya:** They said that the NDA would win about 350 seats (give or take 14) and the UPA 95 (give or take 9).
3. **India Today-Axis My India:** Predicted a landslide victory

Opening Pandora's Box: Lessons of 2004, 2009, 2019

for the BJP-led NDA, which it said would win between 339 and 365 seats, while the UPA was projected to win 77-108 seats. According to the channel, their methodology included surveying about 800,000 people across all constituencies.

4. **News18-IPSOS:** Predicted 336 seats for the NDA in the 2019 polls. Their survey projected 82 seats for UPA and 124 for other parties.
5. **Times Now-VMR:** According to them, the NDA was projected to win around 306 seats while the UPA was to win 132 (with a margin of error of 3 for all projections).
6. **India TV-CNX:** Their survey estimated 300 seats (plus or minus 10 seats) for the NDA and 120 (plus or minus 5) for the UPA.
7. **ABP-CSDS:** Survey predicted 277 seats for the NDA and 130 for the UPA.
8. **India News–Polstrat:** Predicted 287 seats for the NDA and 128 for the UPA.

The actual results were, however, different from the forecasts. The BJP won 303 seats and the NDA's total tally went up to 353. The Congress could win a paltry 52 seats, failing to get even 10 per cent of the seats needed to claim the position of the Leader of the Opposition. The UPA's combined tally was 91 seats, while other parties won 98 seats.

The track record of the exit poll companies in India since the 2004 Lok Sabha polls does not inspire any amount of confidence. In fact, exit polls are also often condemned for being biased, relying on skewed data or improper sample size, and being sponsored or politically motivated.

Assumptions or Over-Assumptions

The socio-political-economic conditions in the country are such that one cannot blame the voters if they decide not to tell a pollster anything other than what they perceive the pollster wants to hear. It is very risky for them. For if a person has voted for the Congress and says so to the pollster, but subsequently the BJP wins the election, reprisals may follow. The BJP or any other winner may extract from pollsters details of all those who said they voted for a particular party that eventually lost. What would follow is plain and simple vendetta in the worst form.

In short, exit polls in India have proved to be a hazardous exercise for both the poll companies and the electorate, which is why the predictions have consistently been proven wrong, with small, stray successes here and there that can be brushed aside as exceptions that prove the rule. The exit polls of the 2024 Lok Sabha elections turned out to be a nightmare for the poll prediction companies. Not only did the forecasts go horribly wrong, the numbers given out by the pollsters also showed an inherent bias in favour of the ruling dispensation. This is unwarranted, as it goes against all canons of journalism and the exit polls ethos.

TABLE 2.4
Exit Polls 2024 Predictions[31]

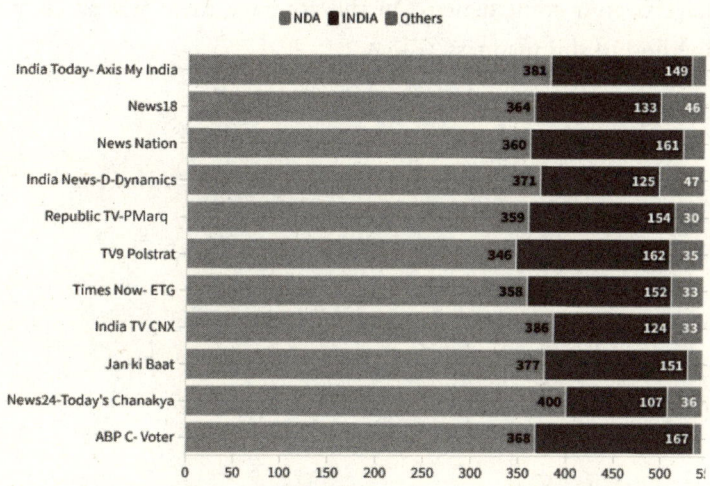

Exit Poll 2024

Pollster	NDA	INDIA	Others
India Today- Axis My India	381	149	
News18	364	133	46
News Nation	360	161	
India News-D-Dynamics	371	125	47
Republic TV-PMarq	359	154	30
TV9 Polstrat	346	162	35
Times Now- ETG	358	152	33
India TV CNX	386	124	33
Jan ki Baat	377	151	
News24-Today's Chanakya	400	107	36
ABP C- Voter	368	167	

There is a lurking suspicion that the exit poll companies and media outlets had made up their minds about the results even before a single vote was cast. Business interests, an unfounded belief that the BJP would break all past records, and the fear of reprisals seemed to have influenced such predictions, which were in no way based on ground reports and realities. The failure to read the mind of the electorate with the help of data analysis and the collection of proper demographic samples was so monumental that the science of exit polls itself came under a big question mark.

Assumptions or Over-Assumptions

Interestingly, in their uniform failure to predict the results correctly, one point of success for the pollsters was that they all, through slightly varying numbers, forecast a landslide victory for the NDA that would surpass its previous tallies. This couldn't have been a coincidence. On the contrary, there was surely a method to this madness.

THREE

Science Meets Social Science: The Theory of Exit Polls

The debacles of past exit polls, overshadowed only by the ultimate disaster of the 2024 predictions, have brought to the fore the questions and doubts that today undercut the pollsters as well as their accountability (or lack thereof) and methods of conducting these polls.

For accurate predictions, the methodology followed in carrying out exit polls is of cardinal importance. On it depend their efficacy and credibility. Unfortunately, however, it is mostly shrouded in mystery. Poll prediction companies keep their methodologies secret from the public. This gives rise to suspicion and mistrust and leaves scope for citizens to spin all sorts of conspiracy theories about political intrigues, financial manipulations and voter frauds. The huge gap between the exit poll results and the final official tally of elected seats declared by the ECI after the 2024 Lok Sabha polls' conclusion has

Assumptions or Over-Assumptions

strengthened the suspicion further, much to the peril of the poll prediction exercise itself. As the head of one such company put it, the failure to accurately predict the general elections results in 2004 damaged the credibility of exit polls for 20 years, so the 2024 fiasco has added at least 20 more years to the cause of winning back the confidence of the people. This is no hyperbole but an admission of a harsh, unpalatable truth.

There are several key components of exit polls, the chief of these being the voters who are interviewed immediately after they cast their votes. They are called responders. Then come questions of data size, responder demography and honesty—i.e., whether the responders' answers to questions about their polling behaviour are true or not. Do they equivocate or evade? Are they diplomatic in their answers? Should one take whatever they say with a pinch of salt? In other words, are the responders reliable enough for the pollsters to base their assumptions on their responses for electoral forecasts? The trustworthiness and reliability of exit polls depend on these crucial factors.

The Science of Surveys

The science of surveys used to compile exit polls works with the help of data collected after interviewing a large number of respondents using a structured questionnaire. The interviews can be done either over the telephone or in a face-to-face manner.

The history of opinion polls that preceded that of exit polls is highly interesting. It is a precise exercise needing

Science Meets Social Science: The Theory of Exit Polls

detailed planning, careful supervision and a great deal of time. The American Dictionary of Campaigns and Elections states: 'Polling is the process of interviewing a relatively small number of people selected from relatively larger population in order to discover public deeper.' The main point is such polls are not impressionistic but quantitative.[1]

Well-known Indian opinion polling analyst N. Bhaskara Rao once noted, 'Opinion polls in the context of national elections are perceived as indicators of not just the dimension of victory and defeat but also the attributes for differences and margins at micro and macro levels.'[2]

In India, opinion polling dates back to 1957, when during the second Lok Sabha elections the IIPO conducted a poll. The methodology followed was so sound that not even the best guesswork or estimate can do without it even today. Only with a structured questionnaire the data can be collected coherently and thereafter analysed systematically.

In such surveys, the sample size and its representativeness matter most. Since the first national poll conducted in India in 1957, there has been a vast improvement in many aspects, especially the sample size. A national sample of 20,000 to 30,000 respondents that used to be considered large in those days is now a thing of the past—outmoded. Today, survey agencies conducting exit polls use samples as big as 10 lakhs. Exit polls of samples of a few lakhs have become quite commonplace.

The method followed by Lokniti, the research programme at the Centre for the Study of Developing Societies (CSDS),

Assumptions or Over-Assumptions

might be instructive. Though it does not normally conduct exit polls, it did conduct a few during the 1996 Lok Sabha elections, using a sample size of 17,604. To its credit, it did make a very accurate national projection for both vote share and seats. It has continued its study of voting behaviour using post-poll surveys as a tool. Its post-poll survey of the 2019 Lok Sabha elections had a sample size of a little more than 25,000. Its seat projections were off the mark on some occasions, but the vote share estimates were very close to reality.[3]

While a large sample size is important, what really matters, as many experts aver, is how representative it is and whether it reflects the various types of voter profiles. If these basic rules are not adhered to, the mere size of the samples may not yield the desired results and poll forecasts can go haywire. However, this has become the norm now due to the pressure on television channels—which, in most cases, are the sponsors for these exit polls—to have the largest sample. Hence, exit poll companies in general use bigger and bigger samples.

With the advancement of technology, surveyors can now use call-backs (returned phone calls) to respondents, images of interviews being conducted, and WhatsApp groups. But there is no thumb rule for getting the predictions correct.

There are other challenges as well. The prediction of seats is based on a model called the swing model. In this method, the poll makes an estimate of vote shares for different parties and alliances by interviewing selected respondents. Then the seat forecast is made based on the result of the previous election.

Science Meets Social Science: The Theory of Exit Polls

Estimating the vote share in Indian politics is a stupendous task considering the country's immense diversity of geography, caste, religion, language, education levels and economic class. Each of these elements impacts voting behaviour. Over-representation or under-representation of any of these diverse sections of voters can take a heavy toll on the accuracy of estimates.

The list of difficulties is long enough. Since the swing model is applied on the previous vote shares, fresh problems crop up when there is a change in alliances or a split or a merger of parties between two elections. Data analysis in such situations becomes a far more difficult and complicated task. Measurement in the swing model does not pose many problems when the contest is restricted to two parties. But the more political players there are in the fray, the further the complexity of swings increases.

The question is whether exit polls can be comprehensive. Some agencies claim to make seat-wise estimates. But the count method that is applied in such estimates is time-consuming and labour-intensive, as assessments are made for each seat. This is when the sample size grows as high as several lakhs.

However, innovations have been attempted by some agencies to refine the count method. This has enabled them to reap greater benefits by spending relatively less time and resources. The technique in such cases is not to cover all the constituencies even when an exit poll may claim to have done so. For example, with regards to the 2024 Lok Sabha elections, there was virtually no need for conducting exit polls in Varanasi, where the Prime Minister was contesting, or Gandhinagar, where the union home minister was the candidate. If the constituencies are scanned state-wise, many such seats could be skipped while still being able to make the most accurate estimate.

When this elimination method is combined with the count method, the survey is needed in a limited number of difficult constituencies, i.e. the swing constituencies. Thus, there are chances of an innovative exit poll being far more accurate than polls conducted using traditional methodology. However, the advantage of the polls using traditional methodology is that they estimate vote share and help in the analysis of voting behaviour on the basis of the voters' different socio-economic backgrounds. The count method, on the other hand, can hardly give an estimate of vote share. Any systematic analysis of voting behaviour is a far cry.

Again, there are many exit polls that merely throw up a number for seats and stop short of quantifying vote shares, nor do they disclose methodological details. This is not acceptable. To call them exit polls is indeed allowing them a misnomer.

Dissecting Differentiations

The time has come to distinguish between real exit polls and estimate polls. For any poll worth the name, a vote share estimate is a must. If this is not done during the poll, it does not qualify to be called so. A poll that does not estimate votes yet predicts

Science Meets Social Science: The Theory of Exit Polls

seats cannot gloss over its imperfections in the name of using innovative methods. Over the years, psephology has become equated with pre-poll surveys and exit polls, which are done by almost all major media houses to predict the winners of various elections.

The adequate number of respondents that should be interviewed in an election survey is determined statistically and the size of the sample does not, to a great extent, determine its quality and credibility. The election surveys, unlike pre-poll opinion surveys in India, tend not to go wrong, as most of the polls have big samples.

However, the flaw in exit polls is that even when the sample size is large, the choice of sampling methods is often unscientific and unable to statistically cover the whole gamut of the study. This is why these surveys are not representative and their seat predictions go wrong on several occasions. Random sampling methods, which are popularly used for pre-poll and post-poll election surveys, have a greater chance of getting a representative sample as compared to a sample drawn purposively.

Purposive or quota sampling of voters is popularly used by market research agencies for conducting exit polls. In this methodology, a quota is fixed for sampling the respondents based on gender, education, caste, community, age group, occupational background and economic class. There is serious danger in following this method in a vast country such as India, with its variegated population characterized by innumerable castes and ethnic groups.

Assumptions or Over-Assumptions

Further, India is a country with almost the majority of its population living in rural areas. This means that in order to be truly representative, any election survey, whatever its sample size, should try to conduct about more than 50 per cent of its interviews in the villages and rural areas, and only about 30 to 40 per cent in the towns and cities. Unfortunately, this is not followed by most of the market research agencies that are engaged in election polling in India. That is not surprising. It is only natural due to the constraints inherent in the task and high costs of conducting surveys in rural areas. Many of the polls suffer from an urban bias, which eventually leads to their sample being unrepresentative. A sample with more interviews in towns and cities is most likely to have more educated and rich middle-class respondents. Thus, the whole sample becomes biased and distorted, making it completely unrepresentative and inaccurate. The survey is doomed from the beginning.

It is not feasible to survey an entire population. This is the reason why pollsters select a sample of individuals representing the whole population. The selection of the respondents in an exit poll is a major step in the process of determining how well their views and opinions reflect those of the voting population. For sampling individuals, polling companies have a wide range of options. But they generally zoom in on two types: probability sampling and non-probability sampling. For decades, probability sampling has been the standard method for conducting polls. However, judging by the trend in recent years of fewer people responding to polls, coupled with the rising cost of polls,

Science Meets Social Science: The Theory of Exit Polls

researchers prefer non-probability-based sampling methods. They collect data online from volunteers on an internet panel. In several cases, non-probability samples have produced results that were comparable to or, in some instances, more accurate in predicting election outcomes than probability-based surveys.

In a probability sample, all persons in the target population have a known chance of being interviewed, the aim being not to leave out anyone. For example, in a telephone survey based on random digit dialling (RDD) sampling, there is a known probability that a particular telephone number might be selected. The great advantage of a probability-based sample is that one can calculate how likely it is that the sample findings accurately represent the full population. This ability to estimate, within a specified range, the accuracy of survey findings has made probability-based sampling the bedrock of modern survey research.

In this method, samples of telephone area codes and exchanges are taken and then random digits are added to the end to create 10-digit phone numbers. The first step ensures that phone numbers are distributed properly by geography, while the second step, adding the random numbers, ensures that even unlisted numbers are included. This is the standard practised by nearly all pollsters. The main advantage of RDD is the coverage of the population. Everyone with a telephone becomes eligible to be sampled. However, the great disadvantage of this method is that it is expensive, as many of the telephone numbers generated are non-working numbers. One reason for the failure of the

Assumptions or Over-Assumptions

2024 Lok Sabha exit polls, as one pollster regretted, was the huge expenditure that polling companies could ill afford.

Another sampling method is called registration-based sampling (RBS). In this method, a sample of individuals is drawn from the lists of registered voters, with which phone numbers are matched. This is less costly and more efficient since almost all calls end up reaching a working phone number. However, its primary disadvantage is that voter lists often do not include unlisted telephone numbers and may have voters who have moved or are not truly eligible to vote at their current polling stations.

Another sampling mode is called self-selected samples (SSS). For self-selected or opt-in samples, respondents volunteer to take part in the survey and as such, their answers may not be representative of the larger population. There are a few types of self-selected samples, including dial-in polls, which are very popular with the media. However, the American Association for Public Opinion Research (AAPOR) has sounded a note of caution regarding this sort of sampling on the grounds that such surveys tend to be misleading if one seeks to poll an entire population based on its results.[4] This explains why pollsters seek to select a sample of individuals that represents the whole population.

Another category is samples from internet panels. In this method, a random sample is selected from among people who have signed up to be members of an internet panel. The problem with this method is that though the sample itself is random, its

Science Meets Social Science: The Theory of Exit Polls

results may be biased, as the population from which the sample is drawn comprises people who have signed up to be members of the panel.

In non-probability sampling methods, the respondents are chosen from volunteers. However, a serious consequence of this method could be that certain types of individuals may choose to be part of the survey with predetermined ideas that could render the final results impacted by their personal biases. This is the most crucial difference between probability and non-probability sampling.

Interestingly, a large proportion of pre-election polls are conducted by political media. People get interested in election forecasts due to the assumption that election results can be predicted precisely. However, the available literature records a series of prediction failures, which is not limited to some specific countries but is a global phenomenon with one or two glorious exceptions, such as the UK since 2005.

On the other hand, in 2019, a team of scholars from all over India conducted a post-poll survey known as the National Election Study (NES), coordinated by Lokniti. It is a comprehensive study of India's general elections from the point of view of social science. It is different from exit polls, which are conducted when voters come out of polling stations after casting their votes. For the NES, voters were randomly selected from electoral rolls by field investigators for an interview in their constituencies before the official results were known. The objective of a post-poll survey is not just to try to understand voting behaviour but also to study the reasons why voters chose particular parties and candidates.

Apart from sampling methods, there are a number of other factors that affect the potential accuracy of the results. One such factor is how the interview questions are worded or whether the sequence of questions presented to the respondents reflects what people really think.

A Ground Reality Check

An important element of an election survey is the training of enumerators who carry out field investigations. This is crucial for conducting the survey accurately. Unlike developed countries such as the United States or many European countries where an election survey is conducted telephonically, in India, an election survey is conducted by enumerators who contact the respondents and conduct interviews in person. As such, for every opinion poll or election survey, the training of enumerators shortly before field investigations begin is imperative for ensuring standardization. The reality, however, is that except for a few academic institutions, most of the market research organizations are known to not spend time on and use their financial resources for fieldwork training and practices. On the contrary, they are known to select one-time trained enumerators from their pool and ask them to do the fieldwork for the subsequent rounds of the election surveys.

The question is whether such training is needed at all. The

Science Meets Social Science: The Theory of Exit Polls

answer is an emphatic yes, considering the nature of the work to be undertaken. Some of the crucial aspects of the training are building a rapport with sampled respondents, reading out questions from interview schedules, using survey instruments, following accepted fieldwork procedures and practices, and using standardized methods of asking questions and recording responses. There are dos and don'ts of surveying that need to be dinned into the field workers afresh for each round of an election survey.

The absence of rigorous training leads to inaccuracies in data collection that sometimes culminate in the failure of surveys. Any data analysis based on it has great chances of proving to be fallible and questionable.

For these reasons, there is a clamour for transparency in spelling out sample design, response rates and the wording of the questions so that these elements can be assessed along with poll results.

The factors behind inaccurate election predictions are found at four levels. There is the socio-cultural diversity and volatility of Indian voters. An important question that enumerators face is whether voters form their voting decisions after the elections are announced or if there is a significant number of voters who make up their mind as to whom they should vote for only at the last moment. The latter are known as floating voters.

The next question that torments the field workers is whether Indian voters really reveal their voting intentions to the surveyors or whether they have to conceal them for a variety of

Assumptions or Over-Assumptions

extraneous factors, including the fear of dominant caste groups and the muscle power of the incumbent party that may imperil their lives if it is disclosed that they voted for the opposition's candidate.

The electoral situation in India is so complex that the concept of exit polls used effectively by and large in the West becomes difficult to be adapted to Indian conditions. There are too many questions to be answered. Experts doubt whether the survey for exit polls can capture the complexities of elections arising out of a multi-polarity of contests, party alliances and the transfer of votes to partners of one bloc, and geographical concentration of votes for some parties in some regions and states. Likewise, Indian elections are often plagued by factionalism in parties, the presence of rebel candidates and local-level dynamics that often become difficult to be ascertained in a survey. Yet, without these components, predictions run the risk of going off the mark.

Another problem that dogs exit polls is the sample selection representative of the demography of the voters and, even more importantly, the nagging question of whether the size of the sample determines the accuracy of the survey. Some experts also doubt the accuracy of various statistical models for seat predictions developed by pollsters.

While using samples for exit polls, the socio-cultural diversity and volatility of the electorate pose a new set of difficulties. Election studies conducted in the past have thrown ample light on the fact that Indian voters are highly heterogeneous, with different socio-cultural practices and demographic backgrounds.

Science Meets Social Science: The Theory of Exit Polls

These influence their voting patterns and preferences, which become varied.

What is even more problematic is that at times, the multi-layered identities of Indian voters—region, caste, community, language and religion—overlap in such a manner that it becomes extremely difficult to ascertain the voters' political affiliations and electoral choices. An example will suffice to explain the complexity: Muslims in a state like UP do not generally vote for the BJP, as is revealed by the election surveys conducted in the state during the past one decade. Nonetheless, there are variations in the voting patterns of Muslims residing in different parts of the state. Muslims in UP do not form a homogeneous group and there are differences among them based on region, language and religious sect, which are reflected in their voting preferences. Thus, a large sample survey may show that certain sections of Muslims in the state have voted for the BJP.

Similarly, the voting patterns of voters in India vary from state to state. This is for the simple reason that certain issues in elections may have regional and sectional appeal and can form the basis of voting decisions. For others, the issues might not have any appeal at all and may not affect their voting decisions. One such latest instance could be the farmers' issue. Though farmers of the entire country threw their weight behind the demand for legal constitutional guarantee for minimum support price (MSP) for some agricultural produce, the issue particularly swayed the farmers of some northern states.

Election studies, done before or during election campaigns,

Assumptions or Over-Assumptions

have revealed that around one-fourth of the voters do not decide beforehand about who they are going to vote for. For this reason, they have been termed as floating voters by pollsters. This group of voters make up their mind during election campaigns. If there is a bandwagon effect, as mentioned in the previous chapter, in favour of any particular political party, the initial predictions can seriously go wrong. There is a practice of pollsters making election forecasts based on pre-poll surveys, with a rider that the predictions can change in subsequent weeks. But their readers remember only the predictions and judge them accordingly after the actual outcome is revealed.

During the UP assembly elections in 2007, a post-poll survey revealed that a large number of voters from the upper castes, who had actually voted for the BSP, shied away from revealing their voting behaviour fearing caste-based violence. As a result, most of the election surveys conducted during that election failed to predict a clear-cut win for the Mayawati-led BSP.[5] Thus, voters who are interviewed outside the polling booth after they have voted do not always open up about their actual decisions. This happens because there is a fear of reprisals in case the revelation of the party they voted for is used by other political parties in subsequently identifying and targeting them.

It is much easier to forecast the election outcome in a state where only two main political parties lock horns and the surveys get their vote shares correctly. However, in states where there are many-cornered contests, making accurate predictions becomes hazardous. A slight error in estimating the vote share of any one party can make seat predictions go wrong. In cases where parties fight elections as alliance partners, the prediction of seats tends to be challenging enough. For it is very difficult to compute how votes are transferred from one partner or several partners to the one fighting as the alliance's representative candidate.

The geographical concentration of votes for some parties in some regions of certain states also poses difficulties for making an accurate seat prediction, even after getting the vote estimates correct. The result of the Karnataka assembly elections held in 2008 showed that the BJP had a 1 per cent vote share, less than the Congress, yet it ended up capturing the majority of the seats. The Congress got more votes than the BJP in the state, but its vote was evenly distributed throughout the state which resulted in defeat with respect to too many seats.

The most crucial element in conducting an opinion poll survey is the sample size and method of sampling. The sample size for any national- and state-level elections study depends upon the level of analysis one intends to do. For example, if one goes about analysing the voting behaviour and attitudes of voters only at the state level, a survey of 1,500 respondents would be good enough. But if one undertakes a region-wise analysis in the state, the sample size has to be bigger, as there should be a sufficient number of cases for disaggregate analysis. In such an analysis, data is broken down into detailed sub-categories, allowing one to get a better understanding of the needs of specific groups of people.

Assumptions or Over-Assumptions

Thus, sample sizes for any election survey depend on the level of disaggregate data one requires for the analysis. As long as the sample size is representative, seat predictions based on even a small sample size can come up with accurate results. On the other hand, a survey based on a large but unrepresentative size will produce a wrong seat forecast.

Psephologist Yogendra Yadav, as mentioned in the previous chapter, has reservations about the use of bigger sample sizes. In his opinion, the bigger the surveys, the greater the chance of error. The method of sampling used in an election survey and its accuracy also play an important role in making a reasonably accurate election forecast. Thus, a smaller representative sample can help make an accurate prediction as compared to a bigger unrepresentative sample. The method of sampling used in surveys conducted by market research organizations is usually criticized for not being scientific enough. This becomes clear when measuring the voting preferences and intentions of various castes and communities. The following example will drive home the point.

In UP, a majority of the Dalits, especially the Jatavas, vote for the BSP, whereas the majority among the so-called upper-caste voters support the BJP and the Congress. On the other hand, voters belonging to the Yadavs are staunch supporters of the SP. Thus, a survey sample in UP should be representative of these castes and communities, approximating the respective percentages of the populations of these communities in the state.

If a sample survey fails to gather the opinion of any

Science Meets Social Science: The Theory of Exit Polls

important caste or community, the election predictions may go widely off the mark.

The method through which the sample is selected is thus crucial for the survey. Most Indian polls go wrong because their sampling methodology is poor. This makes the sample profile unrepresentative.

All the same, it should be borne in mind that a scientific and representative sample does not necessarily determine the accuracy of a survey. In fact, there is no guarantee that a forecast based on the survey will be right. A survey has its limitations, since it cannot capture all the diverse and nuanced complexities of a situation.

Media houses and television anchors in India have grown into powerful lobbyists, using opinion poll findings to forecast election results before the actual votes are cast. That such forecasts have gone wrong on many occasions is another story.

To sum up, the accuracy of sample surveys depends on the following factors:

1. The sample should be large enough to yield the desired level of precision.
2. The size of the required sample for any survey ought to be statistically determined.
3. Those who lack experience can use statistical tables that provide various sample sizes based on the population size. However, in some cases, the sample size depends upon the level of disaggregation, for which data is required.

Assumptions or Over-Assumptions

4. Everyone in the population should have an equal chance of being selected in the sample. Probability sampling based on the random method is the best way for ensuring that everyone in the universe stands an equal chance of getting selected.
5. Survey questions should be asked of the sampled respondents in a standardized manner. This is of paramount interest since standardization ensures that questions are asked in the same manner of all the sampled respondents, and that will enable the respondents to respond accurately.
6. There should not be any predetermined arbitrariness in interviewing the sampled respondents.

An accurate survey should follow some basic norms:

1. Every member of the targeted population should have an equal chance of being selected for the survey.
2. Probability sampling ensures everyone gets a fair and equal chance of being selected and in the process, coverage error can be avoided.
3. The size of the sample to be selected should be adequate enough to achieve the required level of precision. The guiding principle should be to minimize sampling errors.
4. The questions to be asked should be simple and clearly worded so that the respondents can understand and answer them easily. They should also be worded in

such a manner that the respondents are compelled to answer them correctly. This reduces the measurement error, though it cannot fully avoid it.
5. The sampled respondents who are contacted and interviewed during the survey should have similar traits as those who could not be interviewed. This helps in avoiding errors due to non-responses.

The Media Mayhem

In India, popular media surveys began in the 1980s when Prannoy Roy conducted opinion polls during elections to find out the mood of Indian voters. The proliferation of electronic media in the 1990s made election surveys and exit polls popular in India and they started capturing the imagination of the people. Pre-election surveys and exit polls have since become a regular feature over the last one-and-a-half decades. At the very beginning, most of the poll results were published only in news magazines like *India Today*, *Outlook* and *Frontline*. Slowly and gradually, leading newspaper groups also started showing interest in publishing the results of election surveys. The demand for the print media to participate in the trend further increased the number of opinion polls being conducted in the country.

What fuelled this growing demand was the advent of various television channels. As cut-throat competition grew for getting higher TRPs, which implied a higher flow of cash in the form of commercial advertisements, the race for conducting

Assumptions or Over-Assumptions

election surveys and airing them as quickly as possible began. Even today, while election polls are of different kinds, it is pre-polls and exit polls which catch the attention of most people. The reason is simple: people are eager to know which party or alliance is likely to win the elections and how many seats they will win, even before the counting of all votes is over and the results are officially declared.

Exit polls became very popular in 1996 when Doordarshan, the government-owned television channel, commissioned an all-India exit poll. The fieldwork and data collection for this poll was done by the team at CSDS and its findings were reported and discussed in a five-hour programme aired live on Doordarshan.[6] Since then, there has been no election in India where exit poll results have not been televised the day polling gets over.

The history of opinion polls and seat predictions during the last four general elections has been a mixed bag of successes and failures. Why has it been so? Were the polls biased or incorrectly done? Or was there any political interference in showing the results of such polls? Was the sample size of the survey too small for forecasting or was the methodology wrong?

It would be in order to find out how exit polls are misused the world over when a section of powerful media houses, along with their pet journalists-cum-analysts, work in tandem with poll prediction companies to help politicians in their quest for power through the manipulation of the electorate.

Sharon E. Jarvis and Soo-Hye Han offer a brilliant study

Science Meets Social Science: The Theory of Exit Polls

of the issue in their book *Votes That Count and Voters Who Don't: How Journalists Sideline Electoral Participation (Without Even Knowing It)*, published in 2018 by the Pennsylvania State University Press. The co-authors interviewed fifty journalists employed at top US media outlets who have vast experience in covering elections. The book gives a fascinating insight into this crucial aspect of democracy as practised in the age of electronic media. The interview sample started with journalists who wrote for newspapers and wire services including the *New York Times*, the *Washington Post*, the *Chicago Tribune*, the *Los Angeles Times*, the *Christian Science Monitor* and the *Atlanta Journal-Constitution*, as well as the Associated Press and the United Press International. It was then expanded to cover news professionals whom those journalists referred to, journalism educators, online entrepreneurs and also reporters who had left the news business to work in politics. Adding this larger range of news professionals, especially journalists who had joined politics—a phenomenon occurring at the time in India as well—provided the surveyors with new insights into the study of exit and opinion polls.

What one reporter interviewed in the survey said appears to be the reality in India too. He candidly confessed that the way election forecasts were made, it appeared as if the voter was invisible in news coverage.

Scholars have written widely about how journalists identify themselves with the candidates. They are often on the plane with the candidates, so to say, and see themselves as players, believing that part of their role is to interpret the campaign.

Assumptions or Over-Assumptions

Such an overbearing attitude and body language and glib talk often mark many Indian journalists' style of dishing out exit poll figures and analysing them on live television shows. This class of poll pundits has grown larger and become more aggressive.

Journalists are not mere stenographers meant to record the candidates' remarks. Unfortunately, however, news professionals in India are being increasingly sidelined and their role is being played by poll strategists who predict polls, hijacking the campaign news narrative. Pollsters should be held accountable when their predictions go wrong. The failure of exit polls in successive elections in India should be a wake-up call for the media, and journalists should take back their control over campaign news narratives.

Strictly speaking, these pollsters and media anchors dissecting data are not journalists in the true sense of the term. They are commentators. It would not be an exaggeration to say, as is common knowledge, that most of the present crop of media commentators have not even covered a car accident!

In this connection, I recall one Indian television news anchor, who has acquired celebrity status for dishing out his 'expert' views on *any* subject at the drop of a hat, once getting into serious trouble for making a mistake that a trainee journalist would not have done. As a consequence, he was even debarred from appearing on the channel for some time.

The news channel in question was covering the turmoil over the three Farm Bills that the BJP-led Centre had passed in parliament recently. The agitators began a symbolic tractor

Science Meets Social Science: The Theory of Exit Polls

march in the capital on Republic Day to register their protest against the measure.

The situation turned worse and almost went out of control when a farmer died while moving his tractor on the road. The television anchor mentioned earlier immediately announced that a bullet had struck the farmer on the head, leading to his death. A basic rule of journalism taught in every newsroom is that a reporter cannot share sensitive information with readers and viewers without first verifying it with the police and other government officials, unless he or she has witnessed the same with his or her own eyes. In this case, the anchor was in the confines of the television studio, far removed from the actual scene of the incident, and did not disclose the basis of his information. As it later turned out, he had reported wrongly. The anchor had to pay a heavy price for failing to follow the elementary rules of journalism.

The impression one gets from the current media scene in India is that many of the election commentators, including television anchors and psephologists representing poll prediction companies, have an agenda in which voters are no more than some numbers, some statistics. This is because they seem to already know the outcome of exit polls and feel no need to involve the voter. The election forecast coverage has everything to do with their spin and nothing to do with voters or why people should vote.

They have more power than journalists proper. Poll strategists have the money and the sway and they get to tell the public what

Assumptions or Over-Assumptions

to think. They are there to say what they want and phrase it as elegantly or crudely as they deem appropriate. It does not even matter whether it is divorced from the truth or not.

But the real news is the people's stories—their lives, feelings, perspectives, opinions and struggles. As such, it is their choices and votes which have the largest impact on elections. Wrong exit poll projections in India are resounding proof that the people, and not the pollsters, have the ultimate say in a democracy.

How I feel elated to recollect that this is exactly what I did years ago while covering elections in a district far away from the din and bustle of Kolkata. In that era, telecommunications in that part of North Bengal were inconceivably poor.

It would be instructive to recount the painstaking efforts I made touring several constituencies in the West Bengal district of North Dinajpur during a pre-election survey for Lok Sabha polls. I followed a technique that forms the basis of the successful British module of the day. It would help in understanding the reasons for the existential crisis the exit poll prediction industry is now facing in India. Incidentally, the paper I was working for was founded in 1875 by a towering British editor, Robert Knight, who had wielded his pen to expose myriads of wrongdoings by the British rulers of India.

Back then, I had been in the district for three days, during which time I was meeting a cross-section of people other than political leaders to feel the pulse of the electorate. I was using other methodologies including a questionnaire prepared in advance and getting people's reactions to it. I had also studied

Science Meets Social Science: The Theory of Exit Polls

the voting pattern in the constituencies in the previous election. I tried to get a sense of the aspirations of both the new and the old voters and their satisfaction or disenchantment with the party in power. From morning to evening, I toured places and interviewed scores of people from various strata of society.

On the last day, I chalked out my itinerary in such a manner that I could leave Raiganj—the district headquarters of North Dinajpur—after breakfast and travel to Balurghat in South Dinajpur while meeting more people on the way. I was also visiting the offices of all the parties in the fray and talking to the leaders present there to get answers to the criticism of their work by the people. I was so excited to have gleaned a wealth of data from the people and the politicians. Before I had my lunch at Balurghat, I bought my ticket for a long-distance bus to Kolkata. In those days, there was no railway connectivity between Balurghat and Kolkata and we all had to depend on a rather painful overnight bus service.

I made some final enquiries and then headed for the bus terminus. It was quite spacious and filled up with passengers who stood in queues to get into buses going in different directions. I also waited in the queue designated for my bus to Kolkata. That gave me an opportunity to casually talk to some of the people there and test the assumptions on the poll prospect I had made. I was thrilled to find the reactions of the people in the bus terminus reflecting and confirming my conclusions about the electoral fortunes of the parties and their candidates in the district. This last-minute random survey was redundant, yet I did

Assumptions or Over-Assumptions

not want to lose the last chance of verifying my assumptions based on interviews with so many voters who really mattered in the electoral exercise.

I was near the gate of the bus when a total stranger whom I had never met in my life stopped me and asked me whether he was correct in guessing my name. I said he was and looked at him in utter bewilderment. Before I could ask him any questions, he heaved a deep sigh of relief and said, 'Oh, how you have made all of us run after you the whole day!'

I was even more perplexed now. How could I have made someone chase me? And in any case, who were they?

The man then pulled me aside and said he was from the Central Intelligence Branch. Their boss in North Bengal had asked their unit to track me down to pass on a message sent by my boss from Kolkata.

To my surprise and dismay, he gave me the exact timings of my visits to several party offices earlier in the day. 'You were at the CPI-M party office. When we reached there, you had left about half an hour earlier. Then you were at the Congress party office. There, too, we could not find you as you had left before we got there,' he told me with unerring accuracy.

This revelation instantly produced fear in me. As I had been saying different things at different party offices to elicit information, I wondered whether by my frank assessment and relentless questioning I had antagonized any of the political forces. Were any of them trying to throw me into trouble as revenge? The thought crossed my mind and alarmed me. To my

Science Meets Social Science: The Theory of Exit Polls

consternation, he did correctly name my boss, who, he said, had a rapport with his boss. The message was that I needed to stay back in Balurghat for the next two days and cover an election rally there to be addressed by Rajiv Gandhi! That was not part of my itinerary.

I was in the horns of a painful professional dilemma. Should I dismiss outright what the unknown man was claiming to be my boss's instruction? Or should I stay back and perhaps risk being caught in a trap? How could I trust a stranger? He was short, stout and dark with a pock-marked face. Was he part of a criminal gang? I did not like his looks at all and imaginary fears started plaguing me.

I hesitated. If I returned to Kolkata in the bus, for which I had already bought the ticket, and verified the purported instruction from my boss himself, I would not have time to come back and cover the rally. Not covering the rally even when I was very much present at the spot would be an unpardonable professional failure. It would also constitute an act of defiance of my boss had he really sent the message through his high-level contact. There was no way of checking the authenticity of the message with the horribly poor communication system at that time in that remote, backward district of Bengal.

As if to heighten my fear and anxiety, the man said whether I would stay back or not was entirely my call. So far, he had been concerned to save his own job, he asserted. His work was over post locating me and delivering the message as per the instruction of his boss. He also added that if I decided to cover

Assumptions or Over-Assumptions

the rally, he would arrange some accommodation in the guest house of the local municipality which was 'good enough'.

I had no option and decided to go with him. But he did not take me straight to the guest house. 'I will stop at my unit office to relay the message to my boss in Siliguri. You can have a cup of tea and then I will take you to the guest house,' he said, causing me further worries.

I followed him to a one-storied old house by a pond filled with hyacinth. He took me to a room where there was a wireless set. He did send a message that I had been located and that the message from Kolkata had been delivered to me. I was much relieved to find that he had not been giving false information to harm me. I regained my courage and enjoyed the tea and biscuits served by a Nepali cook working there.

He then put me in the guest house. Obviously, he had good contacts with the district administration. Once the formalities were completed, two middle-aged men arrived and introduced themselves as the immediate seniors of the man who had tracked me. We exchanged greetings and the senior-most intelligence officer had a hearty laugh over 'the game of hide and seek' we had unwittingly played throughout the day.

That evening, we had a very fruitful exchange of information on the poll assessment. I found them to be most knowledgeable about local politics. They had had their field staff make a detailed study of the electoral prospects of the contesting political parties. They passed on those findings to me, which confirmed my assessment.

Science Meets Social Science: The Theory of Exit Polls

As I thanked the officers for their feedback, they said they too had profited from my information. 'We cannot directly gather information from people and politicians with the ease that you can. They trust journalists far more than intelligence personnel and open up especially when the journalist knows the art of eliciting information. I am so happy that your findings match with ours,' he said. It was indeed a great compliment to journalism and he was right.

I refer to this experience in such detail because this time-tested method of poll projection that I used can be quite close to reality while predicting election results. What is of even greater relevance now is that it forms one key element of the exit poll methodology developed in the UK by professor Sir John Curtis and statistician David Firth, and has been used by the British media to produce near-accurate predictions for the past two decades. The margin of error in their exit poll forecasts has ranged between 1.5 and 7.5 seats.

Good or bad, exit polls are here to stay in the digital age we are living in. They have become a way of life—an unshakable habit of voters and election watchers. Their main function and utility are to satisfy the insatiable curiosity of voters who find the wait for about 72 hours between the end of polling and the declaration of official results unbearable.

They want willy-nilly to know the fate of their chosen candidates and their parties, for whom the whole nation has just cast their votes. They expect the work of pollsters to be as close to the real results as possible. Different methodologies are being

Assumptions or Over-Assumptions

developed by a whole battery of experts from diverse fields of social and political sciences and statistics for predicting accurate results. It is an evolving process and attempts are constantly being made to make the exit poll forecasts more reliable.

Now, even artificial intelligence (AI) is being employed to make the predictions accurate and bang on target. This is a global phenomenon and each country has to adapt and develop the methodology that is most suitable for its specific socio-political reality.

In the context of the UK elections, one may wonder how reliable these exit poll numbers and the predictions are. The polling methodology designed by academics Sir John Curtis and David Firth was used by three media outlets while analysing the exit polls. The UK has been producing correct exit poll predictions since 2005.

The success of UK exit polls is attributed to the model the two experts developed in 2005. For the past two decades, Britain has been delivering startlingly reliable exit poll results just after the polls close at 10.00 p.m. This is the hour for which the whole Britain stays awake with bated breath. Three major broadcasters – BBC, ITV and Sky – then begin their celebrated show telecast on the night declaring the results of the national exit polls.

David Dimbleby, the election broadcast grandee, recently quipped that exit polls are 'the worst invention ever' because they take the fun out of election nights. The 85-year-old broadcaster said quite a few interesting things about exit polls when they

Science Meets Social Science: The Theory of Exit Polls

turn out to be nearly 100 per cent correct.[7] A leading television presenter, he stated, 'The exit poll is the bane of the broadcaster's life. It is the worst invention ever brought in.' His grouse is that such accurate predictions sound like a thriller which discloses the mystery even before the story progresses beyond page one. What a contrast to the exit poll scenario in India!

However, the reason why it is difficult to replicate the British model of exit polls in a country such as India is that unlike the UK, the Indian democracy does not follow a two-party system. There are too many parties, both national and regional. Poll predictions become much easier in a two-party system than in a multi-party democracy.

All the same, it does not mean that exit polls should be discontinued in India and elsewhere given all their imperfections. They are, indeed, a great tool to understand voter psychology and voting patterns. Glaring failures should not be used as a pretext to discard them altogether, since authentic results are anyway available in a couple of days after the end of polling. That would be like throwing the baby with the bathwater.

On the contrary, efforts need to be made to constantly improve the methodology to make the Indian exit polls as foolproof and accurate as the UK has made theirs. There is no shortcut, no easy way to compute election results on the basis of sample studies in a country like India which has stupendously heterogeneous population groups. Pollsters need to concentrate on perfecting the science of exit polls. It would be a great disservice to the idea of exit polls if pollsters dance to the tune of vested interests in exchange for favours in any form and official patronage. Exit polls should be made a handmaiden only of democracy and not of those who hanker after the loaves and fishes of office.

FOUR

The Fallacy: Shocks of 2024 Indian Exit Polls

The exit polls for the 2024 Lok Sabha elections were an unmitigated disaster. They failed to predict the results accurately, while the numbers they churned out for the BJP-led incumbent NDA government and the Congress-led opposition alliance, INDIA bloc, reflected a terrible bias and a suspected hidden agenda, making a mockery of a tool that can be admirably used for exploring voter psychology with the help of political science, social science and statistics. The exit poll results this time around were so removed from reality that their raison d'être itself was in question. It appears that the poll prediction companies and their paymasters, the media houses, grossly deviated from the canons of journalism, for which they eventually had egg on their faces.

What leaves one dumbfounded is how all these pollsters went so horribly wrong in predicting the results but were

Assumptions or Over-Assumptions

uniformly singing the same tune that the NDA would get a landslide victory notching up 360 to 401 seats. The predicted victory tally was so mysteriously close to the target—crossing the 400-seat mark—fixed by the Prime Minister. It seems almost like the whole exercise was to move up, from the conclusion to the premise, and not the other way round, as inductive logic demands. The pollsters seemed to be hell-bent on fitting their predictions to the expectations of the ruling alliance.

Of all these predictions, those of the three states of UP, Maharashtra and West Bengal stand out as a litmus test for the poll prediction companies' credibility. The three cases together represent the predicament of conducting reliable exit polls in the country. The failure to get the right figures in these three states clearly shows that the pollsters adopted an ostrich-like policy in predicting the election results—they seemingly buried their head in the sand like an ostrich, closed their eyes to the reality, and dished out figures that would sound like music to the ears of the ruling dispensation in New Delhi.

The terrible errors that the exit poll companies made in their predictions in the three crucial states are indeed inexplicable and inexcusable. They caused grave doubts to be cast on the soundness of their methodologies and the nobility of their intentions. Their failure tends to strengthen the suspicion that they did a perfunctory job and simply went by the din and noise the ruling alliance was making about its poll prospects in the three states, without checking the veracity of their claims, propaganda and calculations. Serious questions arise about whether they were actually listening to the voice of the people, or heard it right but preferred to remain deaf in order not to hold the mirror to the powers that be, fearing reprisals that might inflict incalculable harm on their business.

In all three cases, the exit polls crossed all limits of the acceptable margin of error and made it appear as if some political novices and rank amateurs were at work. Yet, this couldn't have been so, since they are all known professionals. As such, the truth must be something else and we must address calls for serious introspection and investigation.

Triple Debacles

The pollsters made the following predictions as part of their exit polls in UP:

TABLE 4.1

Exit Polls 2024: Uttar Pradesh

Polling agency					Lead
	NDA	INDIA	BSP	Others	
Republic-PMarq	69	11	0	0	NDA
India TV-CNX	62-68	12-16	0-1	0	NDA
India Today-Axis My India	64-67	13-16	0-1	0	NDA
News Nation	67	13	0	0	NDA
News24-Today's Chanakya	68	12	0	0	NDA

Assumptions or Over-Assumptions

The total number of Lok Sabha seats in UP is 80. The pollsters predicted that the NDA would bag 69 to 74 seats (i.e., much like its 2019 victory of 64 seats), against the INDIA bloc's expected tally of six to 11 seats.[1] The actual results showed that the NDA's tally reduced to nearly half of that in the previous elections.

What were the poll companies' fieldworkers doing when the BJP could not win even the constituency where the Ram Temple in Ayodhya is located? This seat represents the fulcrum of the BJP's politics. Any professional pollster should have been able to gauge the mood of the people in that constituency and temper the predictions accordingly. It is a wonder of wonders that the pollsters could not keep their ear to the ground in UP and understand the tectonic shift that had taken place in the voters' choice there. In the 2024 Lok Sabha polls, voters in UP, the pivot of the BJP's politics of polarization, showed the nation that they were simply sick and tired of the bogey of the Hindu-Muslim divide being raised before each election for the past one decade. The outcome reflected it loud and clear. The pollsters, however, failed to read the writing on the wall.

Let us now turn to Maharashtra, another bastion of the BJP which had wrested power from the opposition alliance under dubious and controversial circumstances a few months before the polls. The state, with 48 seats, is second largest, UP being the largest. The pollsters were obviously led astray by the hype created by the BJP about its poll prospects. In this state also, they seemed to have made up their mind beforehand that the NDA would be the sure winner, leaving the Maha Vikas Aghadi (MVA),

The Fallacy: Shocks of 2024 Indian Exit Polls

comprising the Congress, the Shiv Sena (UBT) and the NCP (Sharad Pawar), belonging to the INDIA alliance, far behind.

According to Axis My India exit polls, the BJP-led NDA was slated to win 28 to 32 seats, while the MVA could win 16 to 20 seats.

However, the ABP-CVoter exit polls predicted that the contest between the NDA and the INDIA alliance would be extremely tight. The projections indicated that the NDA might win between 22 and 26 seats, while INDIA was expected to secure between 23 and 25 seats.

On the other hand, as per Jan Ki Baat exit polls, NDA was to bag 34 to 41 seats against INDIA alliance's tally of 9 to 16 seats. The seat projections indicated that the BJP and its allies were expected to secure approximately 33 seats, with a margin of plus or minus five seats. The Congress and its allies were projected to win around 15 seats, also with a margin of plus or minus five seats. Other parties were not anticipated to win a single seat.

In terms of the vote share, the NDA was projected to receive 45.3 per cent of the votes, with the INDIA bloc close behind at 44 per cent. Other parties were likely to capture a 10.7 per cent share of the votes.

Maharashtra's electoral contest was particularly significant this year due to major shifts within its key political parties. The Shiv Sena and the Nationalist Congress Party (NCP) had faced splits, redrawing the state's political equations and making the contest more competitive.

Assumptions or Over-Assumptions

The exit polls forecast for Maharashtra was as follows:[2]

TABLE 4.2
Exit Polls 2024: Maharashtra

Agencies	Maha Vikas Aghadi	Mahayuthi
Axis My India	16-20	28-32
Today's Chanakya	33 (+/- 5)	15 (+/- 5)
C-Voter	23-25	22-26
Jan ki Baat	9-16	34-41
Polstrat	25	22

Ground reports indicated that Uddhav Thackeray and Sharad Pawar, the leaders of the respective factions of the Shiv Sena and the NCP, might benefit from the sympathy wave triggered by the betrayals by some of their erstwhile loyalists who had recently switched sides to join the BJP-led NDA. This sentiment could influence voter behaviour in their favour.

The seat-share projections did highlight the competitive nature of this election. Some news reports suggested that because of the split in political parties, the election had become localized.

When the final results were declared, the poll prediction companies had to eat dust. Their forecasts were nowhere near the actual results. The INDIA alliance got 30 seats, the NDA got 17, and the others got one.

The Fallacy: Shocks of 2024 Indian Exit Polls

Such an egregious failure on the part of the pollsters and their battery of fieldworkers to assess the voters' mind seems possible only in the event that they closed their eyes to reality and predicted results that would please the ruling dispensation. What happened in Maharashtra, therefore, was nothing short of a travesty of the science of exit polls.

Let us now turn to West Bengal, where the odds appeared to be heavily against the ruling Trinamool Congress led by Chief Minister Mamata Banerjee. Her government had come under fire from the judiciary—from the High Court to the Supreme Court—for a monumental fraud in the appointment of school teachers. A number of education department officials and Trinamool leaders at different levels, including a former education minister, had been thrown into jail for their alleged complicity in minting money by giving jobs to undeserving candidates and denying employment to worthy empanelled candidates.

Besides this, the government and ruling party had earned a bad name for alleged myriad types of scams, including illegal sand mining, coal field allocations and smuggling cows across the border.

The BJP got a shot in the arm when a Calcutta High Court judge, who had played a pivotal role in giving justice to the deprived candidates for school recruitments, resigned from the judicial services and joined the party. He said he wished to expand the area of his crusade against corruption beyond the court room to the public arena. He explained that being in court, he could take on corruption in high-ranking offices only when some litigants filed cases. But if he joined politics, he could be among the people and take up their causes.

The development had a huge impact on public life in the state. This judge had already won the people's hearts for having taken the lid off the can of alleged corruption at the highest level of the government.

The 2024 Lok Sabha elections were held in West Bengal in this climate of anti-incumbency. The pollsters conducting exit polls predicted a landslide victory for the BJP at the cost of the Trinamool. The predictions ranged from 23 to 27 seats for the NDA and 11 to 20 seats for the Trinamool Congress. West Bengal has 42 Lok Sabha seats in total. The pollsters also appeared to have based their calculation on the results of the 2019 Lok Sabha elections when the BJP improved its previous tally to 18 against the Trinamool's 22 and the Congress's two.

The different projections were as follows:[3]

TABLE 4.3
Exit Polls 2024: West Bengal

Polling agency					Lead
	NDA	AITC	LF+INC	Others	
ABP News-CVoter	23-27	13-17	1-3	0	NDA
DB Live	11-12	26-28	2-4	0	AITC

The Fallacy: Shocks of 2024 Indian Exit Polls

India Today–Axis My India	26–31	11–14	0–2	0	NDA
India News–D-Dynamics	21	19	2	0	NDA
India TV–CNX	22–26	14–18	1–2	0	NDA
NDTV–Jan Ki Baat	21–26	18–16	0–3	0	NDA
News 24–Today's Chanakya	24	17	1	0	NDA
News 18–CNBC	21–24	18–21	0	0	NDA
News Nation	19	22	1	0	AITC
Republic TV–Matrize	21–25	16–21	0	0	NDA
Republic TV–PMarq	22	20	0	0	NDA
Times Now–ETG	21	20	1	0	NDA
TV9 Bharatvarsh–People's Insight–Polstrat	21	20	1	0	NDA
2019 election	18	22	2	0	AITC

But the actual results were a big blow to the exit poll forecasts. Defying all their logic and sample studies, the Trinamool won 26 seats, up by four seats compared to the 2019 elections, and the BJP won 16, down by two seats from its tally in 2019.

Assumptions or Over-Assumptions

The exit polls went terribly wrong in West Bengal because the pollsters seemed to have been swayed by the hype the BJP and different news channels had created about a saffron surge. Had they properly listened to the people on the ground, they could have known that despite getting entangled in allegations of corruption, Mamata Banerjee had consolidated her voter base by doling out sums of money to millions of poor women, mainly in rural areas where allowances of even INR 1,000 to INR 2,000 a month matter much. In addition to this, the Trinamool was more or less assured of the 27 per cent Muslim votes. These two factors alone combined to help Trinamool not only to prove the pollsters wrong but also to improve its performance upon the 2019 Lok Sabha polls.

To understand why the exit polls turned out to be so wrong this time as well, one needs to study decades-long media practices of covering elections.

A Journalistic Autopsy

Before the advent of exit polls, media used to depend on the assessment of electoral prospects of different parties and their candidates made by their own journalists. This was despite the fact that they had limitations in the sense that their budget was small and that they were generally not ambitious enough to make predictions regarding election results. That was believed to not be the task of the press. Journalists toured the length and breadth of the country soon after elections were announced,

The Fallacy: Shocks of 2024 Indian Exit Polls

meeting hundreds of people from various strata of society, including ethnic groups and castes. They conducted extensive interviews so as to capture the pulse of the people: their preferences of candidates and parties and also disapproval of the incumbent government's policies and their implementation.

The methods of journalism proper in forecasting electoral fortunes need recapitulation at this stage before we go deep into the reasons for the egregious failure of the exit polls during the 2024 Lok Sabha elections.

The best possible means at journalists' disposal during the good old days of print journalism was to get through direct interactions with voters a sense of how they were going to vote for or against political parties and their candidates in the fray. That way, they could be in direct touch with the people who mattered most in deciding the electoral fortunes of the country's political protagonists.

However, after exit polls appeared on the scene, this brand of journalism increasingly lost its shine. The author is privy to how reporters and sub-editors in the newsroom today have been doing their job of election coverage rather perfunctorily, as television news anchors, election strategists and pollsters commissioned by different media outlets go about churning out 'statistics' and 'findings' of voters' preferences. These strategists are usually propelled by their own electoral and business agenda. The way the pollsters interact with voters leaves much to be desired.

In the first place, there has been creeping doubt about

Assumptions or Over-Assumptions

the credibility of interviewers deployed by poll prediction companies commissioned by media houses. In many cases, voters are in a quandary about the real identity and objective of this battery of surveyors. They wonder whether they are agents of the government or ruling political parties. As such, whatever they say during such interviews may not necessarily be what they really believe and think about the poll prospects of parties and candidates. Hence, a true picture of what is going on in the voters' mind may elude the poll surveyors.

On the contrary, voters have shown time and again that they have a greater degree of trust in those journalists who disclose their identities whenever asked to. This instils confidence in voters and a rapport is built between a journalist on the field and voters. Once that trust is created, voters gradually open up and speak their mind without fearing any backlash from the government agencies or political parties. I have done a myriad of such interviews and have first-hand knowledge of how bridges can be built between journalists and the people for understanding the psychology of the voters, which is a key component of electoral assessments. Honest, sincere, fearless journalists know the art of winning the confidence of the people and get to the bottom of the truth. When reporters remain objective and neutral, they can easily find out what the people want to say and listen to their authentic voice. If there is trust deficit, truth will elude the media.

Journalists hone their skills in getting accurate information about the people by being in close touch with them, through

The Fallacy: Shocks of 2024 Indian Exit Polls

years of training and field experience. This is how they can have authentic and reliable information. When this expertise is deployed in election surveys, it becomes possible to read the voters' mind correctly and predict how they are going to behave on the polling day and the possible outcome of the election.

I offer here an example of how reporters use this method of dispassionate objectivity, confidence building and courage to fathom the truth with an equanimity of mind in any situation, political or non-political, to illustrate my point. It is from one of my countless interactions with the people.

I was once assigned by my office to rush to the spot of a communal flare-up in a remote village in the Murshidabad district of West Bengal. Two communities had clashed there, leading to the death of 16 persons in police firing. We had no more details on the incident when a sketchy piece of news was shared with the media at the Writers' Building, Kolkata, the state secretariat.

When I reached the scene of action, I found bullet holes on the mud walls of a cluster of huts. They bore mute witness to the mayhem that had occurred the previous day. I immediately started interviewing the villagers present there. An army contingent was patrolling the area that instilled confidence in me to go into the interiors of the village.

The men I was talking to belonged to the Hindu community, which was a minority population living in an adjacent village responsible for the clash. I let them give their version of the incident. As I was listening to them, I could see a motley crowd

Assumptions or Over-Assumptions

of Muslims assembling several yards away. The Hindus told me they were the ones who were involved in the clash.

After I finished my interview with the Hindus, I went to meet the Muslims. That was basic journalism I had been taught since my first day in the newsroom years ago—getting both sides of a story without fear or favour and without letting my personal prejudices colour my vision. I am a Hindu but as a journalist, I always put aside my religious identity and seek to act as a champion of the unvarnished truth.

The moment I met the Muslims, they became agitated and challenged me as to why I had visited the Hindus first instead of 'caring to know the truth' from them. It was a hostile crowd. I retained my cool and told them I had to be in the Hindu village first as it was located before theirs. Just to show them that I was not intimidated by their aggressive behaviour, I told them that had I not 'cared to know the truth', I would have gone away without meeting them.

Their elders understood my point and asked the younger ones to be calm and quiet. Then they recounted what had 'exactly' happened. After talking to both sides, I could correctly reconstruct the incident and found out that the whole thing had happened because of a gross misunderstanding of each other's sentiments.

The trouble started when a *tazia* procession could not pass through the Hindu village. Some tall trees were to be lopped off a little to clear the passage. There were heated exchanges and some Muslims cut the branches of some trees, and a clash ensued. Had both the groups agreed to let the Hindus chop off the branches, the matter could have been amicably settled. Most of the Hindus were not unwilling to do so. Only a few of them were refusing to cut the trees and they could have been made to see reason. But passion ran high and the situation spun out of control.

I could properly assess the situation by talking to dozens of people on both sides. I had no hidden agenda. My only objective was to get to the bottom of the truth.

I suspect exit poll forecasts go widely off the mark time and again because the interviews conducted on behalf of the pollsters have more often than not gaping holes and the contact between the interviewers and the interviewees is too fragile, lacking the expertise of trained journalists. Making reporters play second fiddle to so-called pollsters and their army of untrained surveyors seems to be one of the main reasons for the failure of exit polls in successive elections in India.

On the other hand, politicians at different levels are in close proximity with the people. In fact, they are way ahead of journalists in the art of connecting with the people—the voters—as they have to interact with them round the year. However, a bigger mistake here for the political elites and pollsters is to assume that they *know how Indians think.*

It is indeed strange that the various exit poll companies working during the 2024 Lok Sabha elections did not take a cue from the incumbent party, which changed the gear of their campaign midway through the elections and went on to employ

Assumptions or Over-Assumptions

questionable means of campaigning. On the other hand, the Opposition claimed that it could sense the winds of change and a light at the end of the tunnel.

The pollsters should automatically have redrawn their sample study methodology, taking into account the new development. But they remained confident that the BJP would easily win more than 300 seats and along with its alliance partners, it would come close to its target of bagging 400 seats.

There can be two explanations for this refusal to understand that the voters were not backing the BJP this time around, the way they had been doing so since 2014. The most charitable view would be that the pollsters simply did not have the wherewithal to conduct exit polls correctly in a vast and varied country like India. Yet, it is reasonable to conclude that they have to be in the business and play safe by going with the hype generated by election campaigns. The simple fact is that often crowds at rallies prove to be deceptive. Many of the people attend these out of curiosity to see a charismatic leader with their own eyes from a close range, while in the end they do not cast their votes in favour of the same party. The pollsters failed to understand this psychology.

Secondly, it could be that the poll prediction companies did have inputs about the voting pattern but they decided not to divulge their findings to steer clear of any controversy.

The Fallacy: Shocks of 2024 Indian Exit Polls

A Failed Report Card

Pradeep Gupta, the head of poll agency Axis My India, admitted that their survey had failed to capture a shift among voters in the less-privileged sections of society in UP, West Bengal and Maharashtra, where 170 seats in total were up for grabs and where the BJP lost a whopping 45 seats, compared to its tally in 2019.

'This is our mistake,' Gupta said. He noted that many voters in those sections of society did not divulge their voting decisions for fear of being attacked by electoral workers who did not share their political views. 'We could not predict as accurately as we are known for,' he said, referring to the challenges in capturing how voters had swung in favour of the Opposition, away from other regional parties.[4]

Over 900 people were deployed for face-to-face post-ballot interviews with a sample of 582,000 voters, with the response rate varying from 40 to 50 per cent in urban areas and 70 to 80 per cent in rural areas, Gupta said.

Many women voters asked men in their families to respond on their behalf. This resulted in wrong assumptions about their voting decisions, he said.

On the other hand, the head of CVoter, Yashwant Deshmukh, candidly said, 'We are wrong in 2024.' Their numbers were overestimated by about 50 seats in favour of the BJP amid incorrect projections for UP and Rajasthan.[5]

His disappointment came through in his remark as the media kept asking about the errors his agency had made.

Assumptions or Over-Assumptions

'I wish I could stop giving seat numbers, but that is a professional hazard.'

Election forecasting in India is based on opinion polls, which ascertain the choice of political parties of the sampled electorate and calculate the vote share for each party contesting the elections. The final vote share of each party is calculated by assigning 'weightages' based on the actual vote share of political parties in the previous elections. The weighted vote share is then put into a forecasting model which translates the number of seats each political party is most likely to win, Deshmukh explained.

Pradeep Gupta went to the length of saying that the statistical challenge begins from the very beginning. He confessed correct sampling is a Herculean task and lamented that this was the reason why they conducted a survey before conducting the general survey to predict election results. This first survey is always meant to understand the demographic, including the social and cultural issues along with the local nitty-gritty that end up influencing the results. Gupta further claimed that since 2013 his agency has 'hit the bull's eye in 44 polls out of 47 exit polls that it conducted'.

He also explained how his agency reaches out to the 'right' audience, adopts the 'right' approach to connect with them, and makes a sincere effort to understand them and their needs and issues, likes and dislikes. Thereafter, it collates all the secured information, makes sense of the data and presents it to the right stakeholders.

The Fallacy: Shocks of 2024 Indian Exit Polls

Significantly, he admitted that poll predictions are a seasonal activity and the bread and butter of his agency is its corporate business, which includes consumer insight and consumer trust index, an exhaustive exercise that is run across the country through the year.

This is rather dangerous. If exit polls become an adjunct of other businesses and a means to advance them further using their own publicity, the seriousness of the exercise becomes suspect. Exit polling is a crucial component of democracy and it should not be allowed to be used as a tool for promoting 'main' businesses.

On the other hand, a new and encouraging development has taken place on an experimental basis during the 2024 Lok Sabha polls, namely the use of AI in exit polls. The accuracy in the forecast has made people sit up, though AI is being viewed as a threat to human intelligence itself. Such a threat is still in the realm of speculation and its proponents are advocating its use for the better understanding of life through computations.

KCore Analytics, which uses artificial intelligence, predicted the BJP would win around 250 seats independently and at least 300 seats with its allies. It has beaten all the exit poll companies hands down with its near accuracy. The research firm, which is led by Hernan Makse, a US-based professor, gathered information from people's social media interactions—what they were reading, writing, and responding to on the internet—to predict voter preferences. The analysis also used important data like inflation, which could influence elections. Makse

Assumptions or Over-Assumptions

said traditional polls go wrong for various reasons, including the fact that respondents lie. AI gives a clearer idea of peoples' preferences because it relies on the anonymity of the internet, he said.[6]

Whatever his logic, he has at least brought in a potential rival for exit poll companies with a promise of unthinkable accuracy.

Zee News also conducted AI-driven exit polls with great precision in predicting the outcomes of the recent elections. Its forecast that the NDA would secure 305 to 315 seats and the INDIA bloc would win 180 to 195 seats was certainly not as wayward as the forecasts by the known pollsters in the market.

The 2024 exit polls, however, caused dual shock waves. The first is what we have discussed in this chapter, though it remains just one part of the story. But in a true sense, it was the second reason that really cost them their credibility. As much as we Indians like our politics, politicians and cricket, there is something we hold as even dearer to us: the stock market. The exit polls messed with the wrong pillar of India's being.

FIVE

Of Stocks and Shocks: The Economic Aftermath

One may wonder how there could be speculations in the Indian stock market over a well-known democratic exercise called the general elections. This is not an unknown, uncertain phenomenon that could spur players in the trading of stocks for a bull charge or a bear hug. Normally, electoral exercises are known to determine the fortunes of political parties and their leaders and not the fates of those involved in the money market trading shares. When that happens, democracy is in peril or subverted.

True to India's 'tryst with destiny', the 2024 Lok Sabha elections witnessed a record-breaking voter turnout, demonstrating the strength of India's democracy. However, allegations surrounding the exit polls, market fluctuations and statements made by the incumbent party's top leadership often made this democratic process dubious and dangerous.

Assumptions or Over-Assumptions

To unravel the mystery surrounding the unprecedented fluctuations in the stock market shortly before and after the declaration of the exit poll results, a thorough investigation is needed so that robust safeguards can be instituted to protect the sanctity of future elections. At the same time, it has be ensured that the principles of transparency, fairness and accountability are not undermined by some ruthless and cynical share market operators at home and abroad.

It is imperative to reconstruct the sequence of events that occurred in the share market during the 2024 Lok Sabha elections. On 31 May, the day before the seven-phase polls ended, there was sudden, frenetic activity in India's stock market. The value of shares bought and sold on the National Stock Exchange (NSE) doubled compared to the previous day. Such an enormous spike in stock trading on a single day is very unusual even when there is a big surprising news or development. Consider the following example.

Track the Timeline

The Indian stock market has always been a mixed bag of surprises. Its deep crashes and steep highs have produced many a gasp. In 2014, when the exit polls and general air of the country showed a thumping victory for the BJP, the stock market had one of its shining moments. The stock market trading activity doubled on 16 May 2014. Trades went all out. Yet, even in 2014, it had not doubled the way it did ten years later, during the 2024

Of Stocks and Shocks: The Economic Aftermath

general elections in India.

So, the question that appears intriguing is what was the absolutely surprising, earth-shaking news or development on 31 May 2024 for stock market activity to double. Frankly, there was no such news at all unless one considers the day before the final phase of polling a momentous development, which it certainly was not. In fact, it was merely information that was known to the whole world beforehand. As such, there was no big news to explain the massive increase in stock market trading on 31 May.

The question that automatically arises then is, who were the people indulging in such intense trading without any apparent provocation? Specific investor details constitute private information and are unavailable for public access. The NSE publishes stock market activity by investor categories known as retail investors (i.e., common people), domestic institutional investors like Indian mutual funds, and foreign investors. It turned out that it was foreign investors who accounted for 58 per cent of all the buying of shares on that day. This was surprising because on no day in the preceding week were foreign investors buying in such large proportions; they were simply net sellers. It then appeared intriguing that on 31 May, when there was no big news development, a group of foreign investors suddenly turned bullish about India and decided to indulge in a massive purchase of shares. What happened the next day could offer an explanation to this mysterious share-buying activity by a group of foreign investors.

The 2024 exit polls were released the next day and magically,

Assumptions or Over-Assumptions

every single exit poll predicted an absolute landslide victory for the BJP alliance, some with even 400 seats, a potential first in four decades. But then how did stock market activity double the day before the results of the exit polls were released when, presumably, only the pollsters and their media organizations—and no one else—were supposed to know about the predictions?

When the stock market reopened on 3 June, after the weekend, it rose to an all-time high, driven by the exit polls' prediction of a third term for the BJP with an overwhelming majority that would give the new government enormous power to do whatever it liked.[1] It was with that intent that the ruling party had been persuading voters to help the alliance it headed cross the mark of 400 seats. Evidently, the group of foreign investors who suddenly bought huge amounts of shares on 31 May saw their value rise enormously. On 4 June, when the actual results were being declared, it became clear that every single exit poll was way off and that the BJP was struggling to get even a simple majority. The stock market panicked and crashed. It lost INR 30 lakh crore in value just on the counting day, the highest fall ever in its history. By this time, the foreign investors had sold their shares and made massive profits. On the other hand, the vast majority of retail investors (common people) saw their share value decline and suffered huge losses.[2]

The more technically complex aspect of this saga of apparent linkages between the exit polls and the share market is that there was also enormous profiteering through speculation in the stock markets using share derivatives, through which investors can profit from both the rise and fall in the stock markets. These derivative investors gain the most whenever there is tremendous volatility, which is exactly what the Indian stock markets experienced between the release of the exit poll results and that of the actual results. Data shows there was huge trading in derivatives too, between 31 May and 4 June.[3] Aunindyo Chakravarty, in his independent analysis, laid down his arguments with a careful study of the financial jolts in the stock market.

> The first point is that there was indeed a trigger available in the markets for foreign institutional investors (FIIs) to pump in money on 31 May: India's weight in the MSCI Emerging Market Index was rebalanced on that day. Many FIIs which simply track that Index to calibrate their investments in emerging markets would have automatically bought Indian equities. In fact, market watchers expected US$2.5 billion, roughly INR 21,000 crore, to flow in that day.
>
> It is also clear that FIIs were hedging their bets by buying 31,000 'short' contracts in the Index futures on the same day. Such contracts are bought when investors expect the markets to go down. In other words, if FIIs bought shares expecting to make money if the markets went up after the results, they were also ready for the opposite to happen.
>
> The second indicator comes from the trade data on which segments of the market bought and which ones

Assumptions or Over-Assumptions

sold shares on the day after the exit polls when the markets jumped, and on counting day when the markets collapsed. If on 31 May, FIIs were net buyers (purchases minus sales) of INR 2,178 crore, they were net buyers to the tune of INR 6,847 crore on the day after the exit polls. They only exited on counting day, when they were net sellers of shares worth INR 12,244 crore. So, FIIs lost money, instead of making it.

If anything, it is the retail investor who made money from the market fluctuations caused by the gap between what the exit polls predicted and the actual results. On 3 June, retail investors 'net' sold shares worth INR 8,500 crore, effectively gaining from the big jump in the stock prices. The next day, retail investors 'net' purchased stocks worth INR 21,000 crore, when prices had collapsed. This seems to suggest that the retail investor made the smart choice.

But who are these 'retail' investors? On the face of it, they are small investors with small portfolios. One estimate suggests that a typical 'demat' account holder in India owns just three stocks. This average hides the fact that most of the equities held by this 'retail' segment of the market are in the hands of high-net-worth individuals (HNIs) and the family offices of big corporates. These are the people who account for the bulk of all daily trades in the Indian markets.[4]

Of Stocks and Shocks: The Economic Aftermath

If it wasn't for the exit polls that misled the country and predicted a massive victory for the BJP, the stock market would not have taken such a towering jump on 3 June, followed by that harrowing deep-dive on 4 June. There is no gainsaying the fact that it was the exit polls that induced this desired volatility for derivative investors. The million-dollar question is whether it was done wilfully or unwittingly.

Whatever the behind-the-news story, the net result was that the investors' wealth jumped INR 12.48 lakh crore in the morning trade on 3 June 2024 after exit polls predicted a massive win for the BJP-led NDA. India's equity benchmarks gained more than 3 per cent. However, once the actual results were released the following day, i.e. 4 June, the BSE Sensex tanked by 5.7 per cent and Nifty 50 by 5.39 per cent, leading to nearly INR 30 lakh crore of losses for investors.[5]

Even then, share market sentiments would not have been affected the way they were, since it is common knowledge that exit polls in India are not necessarily reliable. The question is, why then did it happen so?

The answer is quite disconcerting, as it poses a great threat to the country's democracy and economy, something that has never been done or seen in the past. What changed the entire complexion of share market trading were the statements made by key people of the ruling party, along with the exit polls and market fluctuations. It raises serious questions about the potential manipulation of the stock market. The fact that the country's political elites made predictions about the stock

Assumptions or Over-Assumptions

market followed by a sharp rise and subsequent crash does indicate that there might be a link between these events.

The statements of the Prime Minister and the Home Minister on the possible impact of the poll outcome on the share market would make one sit up with shock and disbelief. Claims were made that the market would benefit for a week after the results were announced on 4 June. These statements were seen as unusual. As a result, there was a sharp rise in the stock market after the exit polls were released.

What appears to be a sinister plot is the fact that the exit polls were broadcast three days before the counting day, leaving ample time for the market to respond sharply to the predictions. In such an atmosphere, the suspicion of manipulation only gets strengthened.

The Opposition seized the opportunity to take on the government. Congress leader Rahul Gandhi demanded a Joint Parliamentary Committee (JPC) probe into the matter and the Trinamool Congress' Saket Gokhale asked for an investigation by market regulator Securities and Exchange Board of India (SEBI).

The Indian stock market experienced high volatility before the 2024 Lok Sabha elections. While most experts expected the NDA to retain power at the Centre, the market was nervous amid speculations that the ruling alliance might not secure a strong majority. With exit polls indicating a solid majority win for the NDA, the stock market appeared to have shrugged off election-related jitters.

Of Stocks and Shocks: The Economic Aftermath

With six exit polls predicting a clear victory for the BJP-led NDA in the 2024 Lok Sabha elections, market sentiment received a significant boost.

Market operators started saying that the positive outcome indicated by the exit polls would attract more investments. Experts became optimistic about the Indian stock market's medium- and long-term prospects. A few, however, expected some profit booking after the sharp gains in the market.

With a clear verdict, markets will heave a sigh of relief and return to fundamentals (the business-as-usual mode), said some of the market operators.

Not a Child's Play

It was such a serious matter that intellectuals with proven credentials and political analysts reacted by alleging a potential scam involving market manipulation. These allegations further strengthened suspicion and underscored the need for a thorough investigation.

For example, Yogendra Yadav, in an interview with a news channel that had commissioned one of the poll prediction companies to conduct exit polls on its behalf, expressed concern over the exit poll agencies' 'lack of transparency and potential conflict of interests'. He iterated the charge levelled against these agencies that they do not disclose their methodologies, their sampling techniques, and even the identities of their key personnel. In his opinion, there was a clear conflict of interest,

Assumptions or Over-Assumptions

as most of these agencies are either owned by or have close ties with major media houses, which are known to have their own political leanings.

Yadav also questioned the accuracy of the exit polls, as he felt the agencies might have overestimated the BJP's performance fearing a backlash and, accordingly, deliberately inflated the BJP's numbers to match the narrative being pushed by the party leadership.

Business analysts also took note of the impact of the exit poll results on the share market, suggesting that the exit polls might have led to a stock market rally and the subsequent crash, indicating potential stock market manipulation. One of them wrote that major polling agencies and news channels predicted an overwhelming victory for the BJP-led NDA and the predictions appeared consistent across various platforms, suggesting a coordinated narrative rather than independent analyses.

The allegations of a scam or market manipulation were not without basis, and the question is who could be the possible beneficiaries for whom the poll agencies, as well as the media outlets linked with them, were apparently working. As rightly pointed out by Praveen Chakrabarty in an eye-opening op-ed, probable and suspected beneficiaries can be listed as follows:

1. Individuals or entities with insider knowledge of the exit poll results who might have engaged in illegal trading activities to profit from the market fluctuations.

Of Stocks and Shocks: The Economic Aftermath

2. The exit poll agencies themselves, if they deliberately skewed the results to align with certain interests, potentially for financial gain or to maintain favourable relationships with the ruling party.
3. Individuals or entities who may have used their influence or access to privileged information for personal or political gain.

Now, if it turns out that the exit polls were indeed manipulated, the potential consequences could be extremely dangerous and far-reaching. Chakrabarty has laid down his speculations about the repercussions in the following manner:

1. It may lead to a significant erosion of public confidence in the integrity of the electoral process. This could result in a decline in voter turnout and a loss of faith in the democratic system.
2. The suspected manipulation of exit polls to manipulate the stock market, as seen in the sharp rally and subsequent crash, could lead to significant financial losses for investors and undermine the stability of the financial system.
3. The alleged manipulation of exit polls could lead to legal action and investigations by regulatory bodies such as the ECI and SEBI. This could result in fines, penalties and even criminal charges for those involved.
4. The manipulation of exit polls could damage the reputation of the political parties involved in the matter,

Assumptions or Over-Assumptions

particularly the one which appeared to be the primary beneficiary of the manipulated polls. This could lead to a loss of public support and a decline in their political fortunes.

5. The manipulation of exit polls could set a dangerous precedent for future elections, giving a fillip to further manipulation and undermining the integrity of the electoral process. This could impact the health of the Indian democracy.
6. The manipulation of exit polls could have caused significant financial losses for investors who made decisions relying on the manipulated polls. This could result in a loss of trust in the financial system and a decline in investment in the Indian economy.
7. The manipulation of exit polls could have implications for India's international relations, particularly if it is seen as a violation of democratic norms and principles. This could lead to diplomatic tensions and besmirch India's global reputation.

For all these weighty reasons, it was imperative to conduct a thorough and impartial investigation into what exactly had happened in the name of exit polls and satisfying the people's curiosity about the outcome of their votes before the official results were announced. This was needed for upholding the integrity of the electoral process and keeping intact the people's confidence in the democratic system. In general, potential

Of Stocks and Shocks: The Economic Aftermath

conflicts of interest, insider trading, market manipulation and any other unethical or illegal activities must be fixed and remedied with appropriate legal action in the interest of the people who are the real masters, not politicians and political parties who are only supposed to represent them.

In addition, measures have to be taken to ensure transparency and credibility of future exit polls. This can be done through rigorous methodological scrutiny, the disclosure of potential conflicts of interest, and independent verification processes. The media also must bear responsibility for critically analysing and verifying such information before disseminating it to the public, as they normally do while reporting on incidents and accidents. These are basic rules of journalism that are unfortunately breached every now and then, especially during election coverage.

Thus, one can unhesitatingly conclude from the available data that there was suspicious and mysterious stock market activity around exit polls and election results. As a result, a group of foreign investors gained and millions of Indian small investors lost their hard-earned money which, put together, ran into hundreds and thousands of crores of rupees.

It can be presumed that some group of investors had access to the exit poll predictions before they were made public and profited from this 'inside (mis)information'. This is a punishable crime under securities laws. In most countries, such things would be seriously and promptly investigated.

Chakrabarty, in his astute analysis, raised fundamental

Assumptions or Over-Assumptions

questions that are bound to come up inevitably and inexorably. He asks:

1. Who are these foreign investors that pumped in huge sums of money into India's stock markets on 31 May?
2. Did they act on material, non-public, inside information of the exit polls to profit from them?
3. What is their relationship to the exit pollsters or the media organizations involved?
4. Whose money or on whose behalf were these investors investing?
5. How much did these investors profit in just these two days of trading?

These questions invite a closer look at the case and require a separate query. While we can hope for some closure on these, such chains of events have doubtless sent a clear message to the average citizen: *Yatrigan, apne saman ki suraksha swayam karein* ('passengers are requested to keep their belongings safe').

SIX

At the Helm of Our Fates: The ECI and the Message at Large

In his book *A Grammar of Democracy*, Justice P.B. Sawant rightly states, 'Democracy does not mean only elections and mere elections do not mean democracy as is the common impression.'[1] Hence, the true role of the ECI is not simply to hold elections but also to ensure that democracy can have a full play under its watch in letter and spirit.

However, in recent times, the ECI has come under criticism for some of its acts of omission and commission while conducting elections. It is an independent institution of the country's democratic system. When it is perceived to be buckling under pressure exerted by the executive, it is a sad commentary on the state of democracy in India.

During the 2024 Lok Sabha elections, when the MCC was violated by the elites of the incumbent party and, in some cases, a top leader of the main Opposition party, the Congress, the

Assumptions or Over-Assumptions

ECI failed to act with the firmness that was expected of it. The matter needs to be raised since it is integrally connected with conducting polls and exit polls.

The failure of the ECI to act properly against the political elites for their controversial remarks, from either end of the spectrum, destroyed the level-playing field that the ECI is supposed to ensure during electoral contests. As a result, it tended to vitiate the electoral process. The laws are clear on the issue. The ECI has to exert itself and rein in the offenders, however influential they may be, since laws are equally applicable to both the mighty and the weak. The ECI's failure visibly impacted the minds of the Indian electorate, which seemingly could not depend on any agency for the protection of its trust in the elections.

However, the issue is that the ECI cannot play on the defence that its authority is weak. For instance, as discussed in the previous chapters, it keeps a tight lid on the issues of exit polls. But due to its inability to maintain certain standards of holding fair elections, it opened a can of worms in 2024. It virtually provided a freehand to the parties to sway voters and, in turn, to the pollsters to do as they wished. The lack of trust may have discouraged ordinary voters from divulging any information about their voting choices.

It is evident now that the Indian democracy faced credible threats from a section of unscrupulous investors—domestic and foreign—and their collaborators outside the share market who appear to find in poll predictions an opportunity to make

At the Helm of Our Fates: The ECI and the Message at Large

windfall profits to the tune of lakhs of crores of rupees in a matter of just two to three days. In the process, not only do ordinary people run the risk of getting duped after having invested their hard-earned money in share trading, but the entire democratic process may find itself under attack.

If these operators are not checked through legal mechanisms by market regulators, chances are that they would manipulate the electoral outcome to serve their financial interests. As has been seen during the elections this time around, they would, in all likelihood, try to rope in key political players to stimulate sentiments in the share market to fulfil their design. Both the electoral and economic institutions of the country may be sabotaged by predatory finance capital.

The ECI needs to step in before it is too late. There should be concerted efforts by the ECI and the market regulators such as SEBI and the Reserve Bank of India (RBI) to foil any attempts by share market players and the ruling regime to run amok with the two vital systems of Indian democracy—elections and the money market.

Several reports of the ECI, at different times and in informal group discussions at various forums by experts and civil society activists, have categorically pointed out many flaws in the electoral system of the country. Some of them have suggested remedies, yet the problems persist, defying solutions.

The Joint Parliamentary Committee (JPC) on Amendments to Election Laws (1971-72), the Tarkunde Committee Report of 1975, the Goswami Committee Report on 1990, the

Assumptions or Over-Assumptions

Constitution Bill 1994 and the Representation of the People (Second Amendment) Bill, 1994, and the Indrajit Gupta Committee Report 1998 have made several comprehensive recommendations regarding electoral reforms. Some reforms have been implemented, but it's a job barely half-done. Considering the gravity of the situation, one may say it is 'petty done and undone vast'. An intrepid CEC like T.N. Seshan tried his best to cleanse the system but ended up in failure. His successor, M.S. Gill, faced some problems too. Former CEC J.M. Lyngdoh also found himself in a helpless position but could not provide a suitable remedy to stop malpractices in elections despite his best intentions and efforts. Thereafter, several CECs and ECI members such as T.S. Krishnamurthy, N. Gopalaswami, Ashok Lavasa and Navin Chawla tried in their own ways to improve the electoral process, but without much success.[2]

Finding the Essence of *Janhit*

There is a pervasive feeling that all is not well with the electoral system of the country. Elections occupy a central position in legitimizing the democratic process of a country. As such, the distortions affecting the conduct of free and fair elections need to be corrected without any further delay by making suitable changes in the laws governing the holding of elections. The time has come to put in place some hard rules and laws in the country's Constitution to prevent forces from corrupting the electoral process.

To achieve this, certain measures have to be taken. Justice Sawant outlines a few crucial pointers in this regard:

1. Currently, the ECI has no independent staff of its own; it has to depend on the staff provided by the Centre and state governments during elections. Thus, the administrative staff have a dual responsibility to the government for ordinary administration and to the ECI for electoral administration. This is not conducive to conducting impartial elections. At every election, complaints are lodged that the state administration is not using central forces to rein in the ruling party cadre indulging in electoral malpractices.

   Since elections are now held almost round the year, the ECI should have a permanent electoral administration with adequate disciplinary control over the staff. This would make the task of poll predictions much easier, as voting can be free from tampering by the musclemen given a free hand by the ruling party to rig the polls.

2. The CEC should not be at the mercy of the executive and the parliament for all that they need for conducting polls. They should have an independent and separate department for the sake of objectivity and impartiality.

3. The ECI should be able to provide funds to genuine candidates through political parties, whose accounts should be auditable. This is needed for preventing

corruption and ensuring a level-playing field. The electoral bond schemes that the Supreme Court has scrapped have vitiated the poll process in an unprecedented manner by allowing corporate houses to donate generous funds to political parties, especially the ruling dispensation, without any accountability. This has proved to be a threat to the survival of democracy.

4. The EC should devise ways and means to make sure that the mass media play a non-partisan role during elections.

5. The EC should stop a growing menace of ruling parties preventing the opposition candidates—by force and intimidation—from contesting elections. This is a blot on the country as an electoral democracy.

6. There should be transparency in the preparation of electoral rolls by the ECI, and its personnel entrusted with the work should be held accountable so that the names of genuine voters are not deleted for political reasons.

7. The ECI should devise a mechanism to unearth black money which is pumped into elections to influence voters with freebies.

8. The ECI should apply the MCC strictly and punish the offenders irrespective of the high positions politicians occupy in the government.

At the Helm of Our Fates: The ECI and the Message at Large

To conclude, it would be in the fitness of things to remember the words of caution Justice Sawant writes in his book to save democracy from 'money sharks' who dominate the corporate sector, disregarding the interests of the millions of ordinary and poor working people of India. He puts equal emphasis on making the economic system truly democratic as on the democratic society.

He questions whether the country's precious resources and the livelihoods of millions should depend on speculation when a scientific, rational and responsible approach is insisted on in every field. It seems that today we are more bothered about the GDP growth rate, SENSEX, exchange rate, interest rates, financial deficit, foreign exchange balance, etc. 'The world is presently being constantly pushed by a few money sharks, on the road to consumerism, and it is this small coterie which is ruling the destiny of mankind,' laments Justice Sawant.[3]

Indeed, for the sake of establishing a true political electoral democracy, there is an imperative need to rein in predatory private capital. Society at large has a big role to play in this endeavour and the ECI should be proactive in realizing this objective.

After all, democracy means 'government of the people, by the people, for the people', to quote the memorable words of Abraham Lincoln, the sixteenth President of the United States. In such a scheme of things, only the people are of paramount importance. Hence, the focus of elections and exit pollsters has to be on the interests of the average Indian. Politicians

Assumptions or Over-Assumptions

and pollsters may come and go, but the people remain forever. India has the distinction of being the cradle of one of the most ancient civilizations of the world. It has also built its credibility as a young democracy brick by brick, putting down firm roots into its soil.

The democratic ethos of India cannot be compromised under any circumstances. Exit pollsters and every major stakeholder needs to pull up their socks and re-assess and re-evaluate their methodologies before it is too late. At the same time, it is the bounden duty of Indian citizens at large to hold their institutions accountable and see to it that they do not deviate from the goals for which they have been set up. India's strength is its diversity that enables its people belonging to different castes, creeds and ethnic groups to accommodate and assimilate different views without being cowed down by the agency of violence, fear or misleading facts. Even if most of those who swear by democracy forget the power of the people, the exit pollsters must remember that India is watching.

Acknowledgements

I am indebted first and foremost to two editors of *The Statesman*—S. Nihal Singh and C.R. Irani. Nihal Singh recruited me at the paper. He showed by his own example what fearless journalism means. I learnt the art sitting at his feet. C.R. Irani was a towering personality and he taught us how to wield the pen without fear or favour.

I acknowledge my debt to Sharon E. Jarvis and Soo-Hye Han for their book *Votes That Count and Voters Who Don't: How Journalists Sideline Electoral Participation* (2018), and Justice P.B. Sawant for his book *A Grammar of Democracy* (2013). They have given me new insights into the topic dealt with in my book.

I extend my regards to Rupa Publications for this opportunity and collaboration. I am also indebted to several leading media houses in and outside the country for enriching me with their varied articles and news items related to the subject of my book.

Notes

Introduction

1. Ewe, Kohe, 'The Ultimate Election Year: All the Elections Around the World in 2024', *Time Magazine*, 28 December 2023, https://tinyurl.com/46yuv8pr. Accessed on 19 September 2024.
2. Rajvanshi, Astha, and Yasmeen Serhan, 'A Make-or-Break Year for Democracy Worldwide', *Time Magazine*, 10 January 2024, https://tinyurl.com/2h8zhkue. Accessed on 19 September 2024.
3. Ibid.
4. The *New York Times*, for instance, published an entire series of articles focusing on the undecided voters who were not convinced with either the Democrats or the Republicans. The media mogul is updating its coverage with every debate and registering the core reasons and rationales behind the voters' decisions.
5. Mukane, Pratik Prashant, 'Poll of Polls: 10 Exit Polls Predict 350+ Seats for BJP-led NDA, Three 400+; INDIA Bloc to Get Less Than 200 seats', *Livemint*, 1 June 2024, https://tinyurl.com/vh8nxx2w. Accessed on 19 September 2024.
6. Shamim, Sarah, 'Why Were 141 India Opposition MPs Suspended from Parliament?', *Al Jazeera*, 19 December 2023, https://tinyurl.com/yt936wvs. Accessed on 19 September 2024.
7. 'Lok Sabha Election Results 2024 updates: Highlights on June 4, 2024', *The Hindu*, 5 June 2024, https://tinyurl.com/zcnvy3tm. Accessed on 19 September 2024.

Assumptions or Over-Assumptions

Chapter 1: Dumbfounded: 4 June, 2024

1. Kiyada, Sudev, and Anand Katakam, 'How India Conducted the World's Largest Election', *Reuters*, 6 June 2024, https://tinyurl.com/295srpy3. Accessed on 19 September 2024.
2. 'Watch: Axis My India's Pradeep Gupta Gets Emotional as Results Defy Exit Polls', *India Today*, 4 June 2024, https://tinyurl.com/4umdkx4s. Accessed on 19 September 2024.
3. 'Explained | Exit Polls and Rules Around it in India', *Deccan Herald*, 12 April 2024, https://tinyurl.com/2s35wdkp. Accessed on 19 September 2024.
4. Singh, Richa, *Opinion Polls and Exit Polls in India: A Study*, Indu Book Services Pvt. Ltd., Delhi, 2019.
5. Roy, Prannoy, and Dorab R. Sopariwala, *The Verdict: Decoding India's Elections,* Penguin Random Hiuse India, New Delhi, 2019.
6. Greiner, D. James, and Kevin M. Quinn, 'Long Live the Exit Poll', *Daedalus*, Vol. 141, No. 4, 2012, pp. 9–22.
7. Rai, Praveen, 'Fallibility of Opinion Polls in India', *Economic and Political Weekly*, Vol. 49, No. 18, 2014, pp. 13–17.
8. Singh, Richa, op. cit.
9. Mojo Story, 'Yogendra Yadav's #Election2024 Forecast Different From Prashant Kishor, He Says.. I Barkha Dutt', *YouTube*, 23 May 2024, https://tinyurl.com/y3dy3mmr. Accessed on 19 September 2024.
10. Mercer, Andrew, '5 Key Things to Know About the Margin of Error in Election Polls,' *PEW Research Center*, 8 September 2016, https://tinyurl.com/5n8tkjax. Accessed on 19 September 2024.

Chapter 2: Opening Pandora's Box: Lessons of 2004, 2009, 2019

1. Sumeda, and Sruthi Darbhamulla, 'Elections that Shaped India | An 'Upset' Victory in 2004, and the Rise of the UPA', *The Hindu*, 15 April 2024, https://tinyurl.com/5ydms5bb. Accessed on 21 September 2024.
2. 'General Elections 2004: Facts and Figures', *India Today*, 23 July 2023,

Notes

https://tinyurl.com/2xcjwj83. Accessed on 22 September 2024.

3. Kalia, Saumya, 'A Brief History of EVMs in India | Explained', *The Hindu*, 19 April 2024, https://tinyurl.com/5fmnkvbx. Accessed on 21 September 2024.

4. 'General Election, 2004 (Vol I, II, III)', *Election Commission of India*, https://tinyurl.com/pzbeph3n. Accessed on 21 September 2024.

5. 'Exit Polls: How Accurate Are They? A Look Back at 2004, 2009, 2014 Predictions', *Financial Express*, 19 May 2019, https://tinyurl.com/yc4xzyj8. Accessed on 20 September 2024.

6. 'Interim Budget 2004-2005 Speech of Jaswant Singh Minister of Finance', *Union Budget & Economic Survey*, 3 February 2004, https://tinyurl.com/bdd2vz3y. Accessed on 20 September 2024.

7. S.V., Vikas, '2004 Exit Polls: When Surveys Got it Horribly Wrong', *OneIndia*, 20 May 2019, https://tinyurl.com/mtrc3tzz. Accessed on 20 September 2024.

8. Deuskar, Nachiket, 'Can 2019 Exit Polls Turn Out to be Wrong Like 2004?', *MoneyControl*, 20 May 2019, https://tinyurl.com/2k5v24cu. Accessed on 20 September 2024.

9. C.G., Manoj, 'Explained: How Left Opposed India-US Nuclear Deal, Leading to Split with UPA Govt', *The Indian Express*, 6 August 2021, https://tinyurl.com/r947cb29. Accessed on 20 September 2024.

10. Baru, Sanjay, *The Accidental Prime Minister: The Making and Unmaking of Manmohan Singh*, Penguin Random House India, Delhi, 2014.

11. 'General Elections–2009', *Election Commission of India*, 2 March 2009, https://tinyurl.com/4vvepps9. Accessed on 20 September 2024.

12. Chauhan, Chetan, and Nagendar Sharma, 'Sack My Colleague: CEC Gopalaswami to President', *Hindustan Times*, 1 February 2009, https://tinyurl.com/ysvbcjpm. Accessed on 22 September 2024.

13. 'President Rejects CEC Advice, Navin Chawla Stays', *The Indian Express*, 1 March 2009, https://tinyurl.com/mwxskaze. Accessed on 22 September 2024.

14. Tewari, Ruhi, 'Reds Go Online for Votes, Cash in on Run-Up to 'Young' Polls', *Livemint*, 18 March 2009, https://tinyurl.com/2s4akmzc. Accessed on 22 September 2024.

Assumptions or Over-Assumptions

15 Ahuja, Amit, and Susan Ostermann, 'The Election Commission of India: Guardian of Democracy', *Guardians of Public Value: How Public Organisations Become and Remain Institutions,* 2021, pp. 37–62.

16 'EC Files Criminal Case Against Varun Gandhi', *The Indian Express*, 17 March 2009, https://tinyurl.com/5cfn8hw3. Accessed on 22 September 2024.

17 'Tringing In', *BangaloreMirror*, 8 September 2008, https://tinyurl.com/4f549kax. Accessed on 22 September 2024.

18 'CNN-IBN-CSDS: Predicting The Polls', *Outlook India*, 23 February 2009, https://tinyurl.com/3nv6sb6r. Accessed on 22 September 2024.

19 'Star-Nielsen Poll 1: Poll Gives UPA 257, NDA 184, Third Front 96', *Outlook India*, 23 March 2009, https://tinyurl.com/2erbdhus. Accessed on 22 September 2024.

20 'Outlook India–The Week: UPA to Get 234 Seats, Advani Best for PM', *Outlook India*, 9 April 2009, https://tinyurl.com/mv6c667s. Accessed on 22 September 2024.

21 'TOI Estimate: UPA Ahead, But Only Just', *The Times of India*, 6 March 2009, https://tinyurl.com/4fzyevzz. Accessed on 22 September 2024.

22 'Prohibition on Publication and Dissemination of Results of Opinion Polls/Exit polls', *Election Commission of India*, 10 October 2009.

23 Das, Anjishnu, 'A Look Back at How Close Exit Polls Were in 2009, 2014, 2019', *The Indian Express*, 2 June 2024, https://tinyurl.com/5292u9kz. Accessed on 22 September 2024.

24 'India General Elections 2014', *Maps of India*, https://tinyurl.com/yjh42s4n. Accessed on 22 September 2024.

25 '39% of First-time Voters Back BJP, Only 19% Vote for Congress', *DNA India*, 22 October 2013, https://tinyurl.com/ays5du7p. Accessed on 22 September 2024.

26 'Election 2014 Live Blog', *India Today*, 15 May 2014, https://tinyurl.com/bdhmcruu. Accessed on 22 September 2024.

27 Baru, Sanjay, op. cit.

28 Umar, Baba, 'India's Modi Attacks Ruling Congress Party', *Al Jazeera*, 4 April 2024, https://tinyurl.com/3yfd9ac5. Accessed on 22 September 2024.

Notes

29 Ibid.
30 'Exit Polls Today: How Accurate Were They In 2014 And 2019 Lok Sabha Polls?', *NDTV*, 1 June 2024, https://tinyurl.com/wrc7c973. Accessed on 22 September 2024.
31 'How India's Exit Polls Got the 2024 Lok Sabha Election Horribly Wrong', *The Hindu*, 7 June 2024, https://tinyurl.com/3j7ty4dp. Accessed on 22 September 2024.

Chapter 3: Science Meets Social Science: The Theory of Exit Polls

1 Singh, Richa, op. cit.
2 Ibid.
3 Ibid.
4 Ibid.
5 Sengupta, Somini, 'Brahmin Vote Helps Party of Low Caste Win in India', *The New York Times*, 12 May 2007, https://tinyurl.com/4k4269k3. Accessed on 22 September 2024.
6 Singh, Richa, op. cit.
7 Weaver, Matthew, 'Election Exit Polls Are "Worst Invention Ever", Says David Dimbleby', *The Guardian*, 03 July 2024, https://tinyurl.com/mw79jd7j. Accessed on 22 September 2024.

Chapter 4: The Fallacy: Shocks of 2024 Indian Exit Polls

1 'Uttar Pradesh: NDA Set for a Big Win Again, Predict Exit Polls,' *Hindustan Times*, 1 June 2024, https://tinyurl.com/4n5fzn4r. Accessed on 22 September 2024.
2 NDTV Profit, 'Maharashtra Exit Poll Results LIVE I NDA Vs INDIA Alliance Lok Sabha Election I Exit Polls 2024', *YouTube*, 1 June 2024, https://tinyurl.com/yc7ntwhh. Accessed on 22 September 2024.
3 'Exit Polls 2024: BJP May Beat TMC in West Bengal, Pollsters Predict 16 Lok Sabha Seats for Mamata Banerjee's party', *Livemint*, 1 June 2024, https://tinyurl.com/ycyf74fn. Accessed on 22 September 2024.

4 Kumar, Manoj, 'India Exit Polls Did Not Capture Voter Discontent in Key States, Say Pollsters', *Reuters*, 5 June 2024, https://tinyurl.com/4arwbkc2. Accessed on 22 September 2024.
5 Ibid.
6 'How India's Exit Polls Got the 2024 Lok Sabha Election Horribly Wrong', *Frontline Magazine*, 7 June 2024, https://tinyurl.com/3j7ty4dp. Accessed on 22 September 2024.

Chapter 6: At the Helm of Our Fates: The ECI and the Message at Large

1 Sawant, P.B., *A Grammar of Democracy*, Bhashya Prakashan, 2013.
2 Singh, Richa, op. cit.
3 Sawant, P.B., op. cit.